Spring Cookbook

Over 100 hands-on recipes to build Spring web
applications easily and efficiently

Jérôme Jaglale

BIRMINGHAM - MUMBAI

Spring Cookbook

First published: May 2015

Production reference: 1190515

Published by Packt Publishing Ltd.
Livery Place
35 Livery Street
Birmingham B3 2PB, UK.

ISBN 978-1-78398-580-7

www.packtpub.com

Credits

Author
Jérôme Jaglale

Reviewers
Alexandre Arcanjo de Queiroz
Manuel Jordan
Stanojko Markovik
Bert Van den Brande

Commissioning Editor
Julian Ursell

Acquisition Editor
James Jones

Content Development Editor
Ajinkya Paranjape

Technical Editor
Siddhesh Ghadi

Copy Editor
Neha Vyas

Project Coordinator
Harshal Ved

Proofreaders
Stephen Copestake
Safis Editing

Indexer
Mariammal Chettiyar

Graphics
Disha Haria
Abhinash Sahu

Production Coordinator
Alwin Roy

Cover Work
Alwin Roy

About the Author

Jérôme Jaglale is a web developer based in Vancouver, Canada. He has spent the last 10 years working with several web frameworks, including Struts, CodeIgniter, and Laravel, and doing frontend work with CSS and JavaScript that is focused on user experience.

He's currently working at Simon Fraser University on a prototype of iReceptor, a scientific gateway federating immune genetics databases in order to help researchers answer complex questions about immune response.

I would like to thank Laurent Conin and Michel Mac Wing at Orika for introducing me to Spring in 2005.

I would like to express my thanks to Daniel Sheinin at 7th Floor Media for encouraging me to learn more about Spring in 2007. It resulted in *Spring MVC Fast Tutorial*, the most popular tutorial on `http://jeromejaglale.com`.

I would also like to thank Brian Corrie at IRMACS for giving me some time to work on this book.

I am grateful to Ajinkya Paranjape and the Packt Publishing staff for their hard work.

I would like to express my gratitude to everyone else indirectly related to the making of this book: my parents, family, co-workers, and friends.

About the Reviewers

Alexandre Arcanjo de Queiroz is a Brazilian software developer who graduated from the Faculty of Technology of Sao Paulo, a renowned institution in his country. He has experience in developing backend and frontend applications using the Java EE platform in the Unix environment.

Currently, he is working at Geofusion. It is the leader in geomarketing in Brazil and offers an online platform called OnMaps, which is indispensable for companies seeking expansion and assistance in more accurate decision making.

> I would like to thank my family who support me in every moment of my life and my friends who believe in my potential.

Stanojko Markovik is an accomplished software engineer, team leader, and solutions architect.

Although he is versatile in many technologies across the board, he specializes in Spring for enterprise apps and Android for mobile.

He's keen on building high-performance applications that are optimized in all layers and are used by millions of users across all continents.

He's currently working at Dashlane, building the best password manager in the world in order to rid users of their need to enter another password ever again. The app he is building has been featured on the Google Play Store multiple times and is used by millions of users.

Stanojko was also the technical reviewer for *Instant Spring for Android Starter,* a book that explains how to use the Spring framework on the Android platform.

Bert Van den Brande is a passionate developer with almost 15 years of experience in the software consultancy world. He has been working in the telecoms industry for the last 4 years. He started his career as a Java and Smalltalk developer. For the last half a decade, his focus has been on Java, Groovy, and team coaching.

www.PacktPub.com

Support files, eBooks, discount offers, and more

For support files and downloads related to your book, please visit www.PacktPub.com.

Did you know that Packt offers eBook versions of every book published, with PDF and ePub files available? You can upgrade to the eBook version at www.PacktPub.com and as a print book customer, you are entitled to a discount on the eBook copy. Get in touch with us at service@packtpub.com for more details.

At www.PacktPub.com, you can also read a collection of free technical articles, sign up for a range of free newsletters and receive exclusive discounts and offers on Packt books and eBooks.

https://www2.packtpub.com/books/subscription/packtlib

Do you need instant solutions to your IT questions? PacktLib is Packt's online digital book library. Here, you can search, access, and read Packt's entire library of books.

Why Subscribe?

- ▶ Fully searchable across every book published by Packt
- ▶ Copy and paste, print, and bookmark content
- ▶ On demand and accessible via a web browser

Free Access for Packt account holders

If you have an account with Packt at www.PacktPub.com, you can use this to access PacktLib today and view 9 entirely free books. Simply use your login credentials for immediate access.

Table of Contents

Preface

Web development with Java has a high learning curve compared to Ruby on Rails, Django, and modern PHP frameworks. Spring, the most used Java framework for web development, makes it as easy as it can get, especially with its recent move of using plain Java classes instead of XML files for configuration classes for configuration. This book focuses on getting you up and running with Spring 4 in the most efficient manner.

What this book covers

Chapter 1, *Creating a Spring Application*, covers the installation of Java and other software on Mac OS, Ubuntu, and Windows. It also explains how to build a Spring application and a Spring web application.

Chapter 2, *Defining Beans and Using Dependency Injection*, introduces Spring beans and demonstrates how to define and use them.

Chapter 3, *Using Controllers and Views*, describes how to create controller methods, use JSP views, and build page templates and multilingual pages.

Chapter 4, *Querying a Database*, explains how to interact with a database using JDBC and how to integrate Hibernate into a Spring application.

Chapter 5, *Using Forms*, describes how to initialize a form, retrieve the form data when the form is submitted, and elaborates on the use of forms widgets (text fields, select fields, and so on).

Chapter 6, *Managing Security*, introduces Spring Security and demonstrates how to perform user authentication and user authorization, and how to configure HTTPS.

Chapter 7, *Unit Testing*, introduces unit testing with JUnit and TestNG and explains how to test Spring applications.

Chapter 8, *Running Batch Jobs*, details how batch jobs work with Spring and explains how to build batch jobs and execute them from a web application or from the command line.

Chapter 9, *Handling Mobiles and Tablets*, explains how to make a Spring web application display different content based on the type of device accessing it.

Chapter 10, *Connecting to Facebook and Twitter*, explains how to access a Facebook or Twitter account in order to fetch some existing data or to create new data (tweets, posts, and so on).

Chapter 11, *Using the Java RMI, HTTP Invoker, Hessian, and REST*, covers how a Spring application can interact with other pieces of software over the network using various technologies.

Chapter 12, *Using Aspect-oriented Programming*, explains what AOP (aspect-oriented programming) is, how it can be used with Spring, and covers several of its common uses.

What you need for this book

You would need a computer with Mac OS, Ubuntu, and Windows. To build Spring applications, you will need at least Java. *Chapter 1*, *Creating a Spring Application*, covers the installation of Java, Maven, Tomcat, and Eclipse on each OS.

Who this book is for

This book is for you if you have some experience with Java and web development (not necessarily in Java) and want to become proficient quickly with Spring.

Sections

In this book, you will find several headings that appear frequently (Getting ready, How to do it, How it works, There's more, and See also).

To give clear instructions on how to complete a recipe, we use these sections as follows:

Getting ready

This section describes how to set up your project for the recipe.

How to do it...

This section contains the steps required to follow the recipe.

How it works...

This section usually consists of a detailed explanation of what happened in the previous section.

There's more...

This section consists of additional information about the recipe in order to make you more knowledgeable about the recipe.

See also

This section provides helpful links to other useful information related to the recipe.

Conventions

In this book, you will find a number of text styles that distinguish between different kinds of information. Here are some examples of these styles and an explanation of their meaning.

Code words in text, database table names, folder names, filenames, file extensions, pathnames, dummy URLs, user input, and Twitter handles are shown as follows: "We can include other contexts through the use of the `include` directive."

A block of code is set as follows:

```
public String userList() {
  return "userList";
}
```

When we wish to draw your attention to a particular part of a code block, the relevant lines or items are set in bold:

```
public String userList() {
  return "userList";
}
```

New terms and **important words** are shown in bold. Words that you see on the screen, for example, in menus or dialog boxes, appear in the text like this: " Under **Maven**, select **Maven Project** and click on **Next >**."

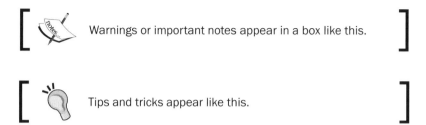

Warnings or important notes appear in a box like this.

Tips and tricks appear like this.

Reader feedback

Feedback from our readers is always welcome. Let us know what you think about this book—what you liked or disliked. Reader feedback is important for us as it helps us develop titles that you will really get the most out of.

To send us general feedback, simply e-mail feedback@packtpub.com, and mention the book's title in the subject of your message.

If there is a topic that you have expertise in and you are interested in either writing or contributing to a book, see our author guide at www.packtpub.com/authors.

Customer support

Now that you are the proud owner of a Packt book, we have a number of things to help you to get the most from your purchase.

Downloading the example code

You can download the example code files from your account at http://www.packtpub.com for all the Packt Publishing books you have purchased. If you purchased this book elsewhere, you can visit http://www.packtpub.com/support and register to have the files e-mailed directly to you.

Errata

Although we have taken every care to ensure the accuracy of our content, mistakes do happen. If you find a mistake in one of our books—maybe a mistake in the text or the code—we would be grateful if you could report this to us. By doing so, you can save other readers from frustration and help us improve subsequent versions of this book. If you find any errata, please report them by visiting `http://www.packtpub.com/submit-errata`, selecting your book, clicking on the **Errata Submission Form** link, and entering the details of your errata. Once your errata are verified, your submission will be accepted and the errata will be uploaded to our website or added to any list of existing errata under the Errata section of that title.

To view the previously submitted errata, go to `https://www.packtpub.com/books/content/support` and enter the name of the book in the search field. The required information will appear under the **Errata** section.

Piracy

Piracy of copyrighted material on the Internet is an ongoing problem across all media. At Packt, we take the protection of our copyright and licenses very seriously. If you come across any illegal copies of our works in any form on the Internet, please provide us with the location address or website name immediately so that we can pursue a remedy.

Please contact us at `copyright@packtpub.com` with a link to the suspected pirated material.

We appreciate your help in protecting our authors and our ability to bring you valuable content.

Questions

If you have a problem with any aspect of this book, you can contact us at `questions@packtpub.com`, and we will do our best to address the problem.

1
Creating a Spring Application

In this chapter, we will cover the following recipes:

- Installing Java, Maven, Tomcat, and Eclipse on Mac OS
- Installing Java, Maven, Tomcat, and Eclipse on Ubuntu
- Installing Java, Maven, Tomcat, and Eclipse on Windows
- Creating a Spring web application
- Running a Spring web application
- Using Spring in a standard Java application

Introduction

In this chapter, we will first cover the installation of some of the tools for Spring development:

- **Java**: Spring is a Java framework.
- **Maven**: This is a build tool similar to Ant. It makes it easy to add Spring libraries to a project. Gradle is another option as a build tool.
- **Tomcat**: This is a web server for Java web applications. You can also use JBoss, Jetty, GlassFish, or WebSphere.
- **Eclipse**: This is an IDE. You can also use NetBeans, IntelliJ IDEA, and so on.

Then, we will build a Spring web application and run it with Tomcat.

Finally, we'll see how Spring can also be used in a standard Java application (not a web application).

Installing Java, Maven, Tomcat, and Eclipse on Mac OS

We will first install Java 8 because it's not installed by default on Mac OS 10.9 or higher version. Then, we will install Maven 3, a build tool similar to Ant, to manage the external Java libraries that we will use (Spring, Hibernate, and so on). Maven 3 also compiles source files and generates JAR and WAR files. We will also install Tomcat 8, a popular web server for Java web applications, which we will use throughout this book. JBoss, Jetty, GlassFish, or WebSphere could be used instead. Finally, we will install the Eclipse IDE, but you could also use NetBeans, IntelliJ IDEA, and so on.

How to do it...

Install Java first, then Maven, Tomcat, and Eclipse.

Installing Java

1. Download Java from the Oracle website `http://oracle.com`. In the Java SE downloads section, choose the Java SE 8 SDK. Select **Accept the License Agreement** and download the **Mac OS X x64** package. The direct link to the page is `http://www.oracle.com/technetwork/java/javase/downloads/jdk8-downloads-2133151.html`.

Product / File Description	File Size	Download
Linux x86	146.84 MB	jdk-8u40-linux-i586.rpm
Linux x86	166.85 MB	jdk-8u40-linux-i586.tar.gz
Linux x64	145.14 MB	jdk-8u40-linux-x64.rpm
Linux x64	165.17 MB	jdk-8u40-linux-x64.tar.gz
Mac OS X x64	221.9 MB	jdk-8u40-macosx-x64.dmg
Solaris SPARC 64-bit (SVR4 package)	139.09 MB	jdk-8u40-solaris-sparcv9.tar.Z

2. Open the downloaded file, launch it, and complete the installation.

3. In your `~/.bash_profile` file, set the `JAVA_HOME` environment variable. Change `jdk1.8.0_40.jdk` to the actual folder name on your system (this depends on the version of Java you are using, which is updated regularly):

```
export JAVA_HOME="/Library/Java/JavaVirtualMachines/
jdk1.8.0_40.jdk/Contents/Home"
```

4. Open a new terminal and test whether it's working:

```
$ java -version
java version "1.8.0_40"
Java(TM) SE Runtime Environment (build 1.8.0_40-b26)
Java HotSpot(TM) 64-Bit Server VM (build 25.40-b25, mixed mode)
```

Installing Maven

1. Download Maven from the Apache website `http://maven.apache.org/download.cgi`. Choose the **Binary zip** file of the current stable version:

⬦ Maven 3.3.1	
This is the current stable version of Maven.	
	Link
Maven 3.3.1 (Binary tar.gz)	apache-maven-3.3.1-bin.tar.gz
Maven 3.3.1 (Binary zip)	apache-maven-3.3.1-bin.zip
Maven 3.3.1 (Source tar.gz)	apache-maven-3.3.1-src.tar.gz
Maven 3.3.1 (Source zip)	apache-maven-3.3.1-src.zip
Release Notes	3.3.1
Release Reference Documentation	3.3.1

2. Uncompress the downloaded file and move the extracted folder to a convenient location (for example, `~/bin`).

3. In your `~/.bash_profile` file, add a MAVEN HOME environment variable pointing to that folder. For example:

```
export MAVEN_HOME=~/bin/apache-maven-3.3.1
```

4. Add the `bin` subfolder to your PATH environment variable:

```
export PATH=$PATH:$MAVEN_HOME/bin
```

5. Open a new terminal and test whether it's working:

```
$ mvn -v
Apache Maven 3.3.1 (12a6b3...
Maven home: /Users/jerome/bin/apache-maven-3.3.1
Java version: 1.8.0_40, vendor: Oracle Corporation
Java home: /Library/Java/JavaVirtualMachines/jdk1.8.0_...
Default locale: en_US, platform encoding: UTF-8
OS name: "mac os x", version: "10.9.5", arch... …
```

Installing Tomcat

1. Download Tomcat from the Apache website `http://tomcat.apache.org/download-80.cgi` and choose the **Core** binary distribution.

> ### 8.0.20
>
> Please see the <u>README</u> file for packaging information. It explains what
>
> **Binary Distributions**
>
> - Core:
>   - <u>zip</u> (<u>pgp</u>, <u>md5</u>, <u>sha1</u>)
>   - <u>tar.gz</u> (<u>pgp</u>, <u>md5</u>, <u>sha1</u>)
>   - <u>32-bit Windows zip</u> (<u>pgp</u>, <u>md5</u>, <u>sha1</u>)
>   - <u>64-bit Windows zip</u> (<u>pgp</u>, <u>md5</u>, <u>sha1</u>)
>   - <u>64-bit Itanium Windows zip</u> (<u>pgp</u>, <u>md5</u>, <u>sha1</u>)
>   - <u>32-bit/64-bit Windows Service Installer</u> (<u>pgp</u>, <u>md5</u>, <u>sha1</u>)
> - Full documentation:
>   - <u>tar.gz</u> (<u>pgp</u>, <u>md5</u>, <u>sha1</u>)
> - Deployer:

2. Uncompress the downloaded file and move the extracted folder to a convenient location (for example, `~/bin`).

3. Make the scripts in the `bin` subfolder executable:

   ```
   chmod +x bin/*.sh
   ```

4. Launch Tomcat using the `catalina.sh` script:

   ```
   $ bin/catalina.sh run
   Using CATALINA_BASE:   /Users/jerome/bin/apache-tomcat-7.0.54
   ...
   INFO: Server startup in 852 ms
   ```

5. Tomcat runs on the `8080` port by default. In a web browser, go to `http://localhost:8080/` to check whether it's working.

Installing Eclipse

1. Download Eclipse from `http://www.eclipse.org/downloads/`. Choose the **Mac OS X 64 Bit** version of **Eclipse IDE for Java EE Developers**.

 Eclipse IDE for Java EE Developers, 253 MB
Downloaded 352,313 Times

Tools for Java developers creating Java EE and Web applications, including a Java IDE, tools for Java EE, JPA, JSF, Mylyn...

 Mac OS X 32 Bit
Mac OS X 64 Bit

2. Uncompress the downloaded file and move the extracted folder to a convenient location (for example, `~/bin`).

3. Launch Eclipse by executing the `eclipse` binary:

```
./eclipse
```

There's more...

Tomcat can be run as a background process using these two scripts:

```
bin/startup.sh
bin/shutdown.sh
```

On a development machine, it's convenient to put Tomcat's folder somewhere in the home directory (for example, `~/bin`) so that its contents can be updated without root privileges.

Installing Java, Maven, Tomcat, and Eclipse on Ubuntu

We will first install Java 8. Then, we will install Maven 3, a build tool similar to Ant, to manage the external Java libraries that we will use (Spring, Hibernate, so on). Maven 3 also compiles source files and generates JAR and WAR files. We will also install Tomcat 8, a popular web server for Java web applications, which we will use throughout this book. JBoss, Jetty, GlassFish, or WebSphere could be used instead. Finally, we will install the Eclipse IDE, but you could also use NetBeans, IntelliJ IDEA, and so on.

How to do it...

Install Java first, then Maven, Tomcat, and Eclipse.

Installing Java

1. Add this **PPA** (**Personal Package Archive**):

```
sudo add-apt-repository -y ppa:webupd8team/java
```

2. Refresh the list of the available packages:

```
sudo apt-get update
```

3. Download and install Java 8:

```
sudo apt-get install -y oracle-java8-installer
```

4. Test whether it's working:

```
$ java -version
java version "1.8.0_40"
Java(TM) SE Runtime Environment (build 1.8.0_40-b25)
Java HotSpot(TM) 64-Bit Server VM (build 25.40-b25...
```

Installing Maven

1. Download Maven from the Apache website `http://maven.apache.org/download.cgi`. Choose the **Binary zip** file of the current stable version:

⊞ Maven 3.3.1		
This is the current stable version of Maven.		
		Link
Maven 3.3.1 (Binary tar.gz)		apache-maven-3.3.1-bin.tar.gz
Maven 3.3.1 (Binary zip)		apache-maven-3.3.1-bin.zip
Maven 3.3.1 (Source tar.gz)		apache-maven-3.3.1-src.tar.gz
Maven 3.3.1 (Source zip)		apache-maven-3.3.1-src.zip
Release Notes		3.3.1
Release Reference Documentation		3.3.1

2. Uncompress the downloaded file and move the resulting folder to a convenient location (for example, `~/bin`).

3. In your `~/.bash_profile` file, add a `MAVEN_HOME` environment variable pointing to that folder. For example:

```
export MAVEN_HOME=~/bin/apache-maven-3.3.1
```

4. Add the `bin` subfolder to your `PATH` environment variable:

```
export PATH=$PATH:$MAVEN_HOME/bin
```

5. Open a new terminal and test whether it's working:

```
$ mvn -v
Apache Maven 3.3.1 (12a6b3...
Maven home: /home/jerome/bin/apache-maven-3.3.1
Java version: 1.8.0_40, vendor: Oracle Corporation
...
```

Installing Tomcat

1. Download Tomcat from the Apache website `http://tomcat.apache.org/download-80.cgi` and choose the **Core** binary distribution.

8.0.20

Please see the README file for packaging information. It explains what

Binary Distributions

- Core:
  - zip (pgp, md5, sha1)
  - tar.gz (pgp, md5, sha1)
  - 32-bit Windows zip (pgp, md5, sha1)
  - 64-bit Windows zip (pgp, md5, sha1)
  - 64-bit Itanium Windows zip (pgp, md5, sha1)
  - 32-bit/64-bit Windows Service Installer (pgp, md5, sha1)
- Full documentation:
  - tar.gz (pgp, md5, sha1)
- Deployer:

---

2. Uncompress the downloaded file and move the extracted folder to a convenient location (for example, `~/bin`).

3. Make the scripts in the `bin` subfolder executable:

    `chmod +x bin/*.sh`

4. Launch Tomcat using the `catalina.sh` script:

    ```
    $ bin/catalina.sh run
    Using CATALINA_BASE:   /Users/jerome/bin/apache-tomcat-7.0.54
    ...
    INFO: Server startup in 852 ms
    ```

5. Tomcat runs on the 8080 port by default. Go to `http://localhost:8080/` to check whether it's working.

Installing Eclipse

1. Download Eclipse from `http://www.eclipse.org/downloads/`. Choose the **Linux 64 Bit** version of **Eclipse IDE for Java EE Developers**.

Eclipse IDE for Java EE Developers, 253 MB
Downloaded 354,015 Times

Tools for Java developers creating Java EE and Web applications, including a
Java IDE, tools for Java EE, JPA, JSF, Mylyn...

Linux 32 Bit
Linux 64 Bit

2. Uncompress the downloaded file and move the extracted folder to a convenient location (for example, `~/bin`).

3. Launch Eclipse by executing the `eclipse` binary:

```
./eclipse
```

There's more...

Tomcat can be run as a background process using these two scripts:

```
bin/startup.sh
bin/shutdown.sh
```

On a development machine, it's convenient to put Tomcat's folder somewhere in the home directory (for example, `~/bin`) so that its contents can be updated without root privileges.

Installing Java, Maven, Tomcat, and Eclipse on Windows

We will first install Java 8. Then, we will install Maven 3, a build tool similar to Ant, to manage the external Java libraries that we will use (Spring, Hibernate, and so on). Maven 3 also compiles source files and generates JAR and WAR files. We will also install Tomcat 8, a popular web server for Java web applications, which we will use throughout this book. JBoss, Jetty, GlassFish, or WebSphere could be used instead. Finally, we will install the Eclipse IDE, but you could also use NetBeans, IntelliJ IDEA, and so on.

How to do it...

Install Java first, then Maven, Tomcat, and Eclipse.

Installing Java

1. Download Java from the Oracle website `http://oracle.com`. In the Java
   SE downloads section, choose the Java SE 8 SDK. Select **Accept the License
   Agreement** and download the **Windows x64** package. The direct link to the page is
   `http://www.oracle.com/technetwork/java/javase/downloads/jdk8-downloads-2133151.html`.

Product / File Description	File Size	Download
Linux x86	146.84 MB	jdk-8u40-linux-i586.rpm
Linux x86	166.85 MB	jdk-8u40-linux-i586.tar.gz
Linux x64	145.14 MB	jdk-8u40-linux-x64.rpm
Linux x64	165.17 MB	jdk-8u40-linux-x64.tar.gz
Mac OS X x64	221.91 MB	jdk-8u40-macosx-x64.dmg
Solaris SPARC 64-bit (SVR4 package)	139.09 MB	jdk-8u40-solaris-sparcv9.tar.Z
Solaris SPARC 64-bit	98.68 MB	jdk-8u40-solaris-sparcv9.tar.gz
Solaris x64 (SVR4 package)	130.57 MB	jdk-8u40-solaris-x64.tar.Z
Solaris x64	89.91 MB	jdk-8u40-solaris-x64.tar.gz
Windows x86	175.71 MB	jdk-8u40-windows-i586.exe
Windows x64	180.19 MB	jdk-8u40-windows-x64.exe

Java SE Development Kit 8u40 — You must accept the Oracle Binary Code License Agreement for Java SE to download this software. ○ Accept License Agreement ⊙ Decline License Agreement

2. Open the downloaded file, launch it, and complete the installation.

3. Navigate to **Control Panel | System and Security | System | Advanced system
   settings | Environment Variables...**.

4. Add a JAVA_HOME system variable with the C:\Program Files\Java\ jdk1.8.0_40 value. Change jdk1.8.0_40 to the actual folder name on your system (this depends on the version of Java, which is updated regularly).

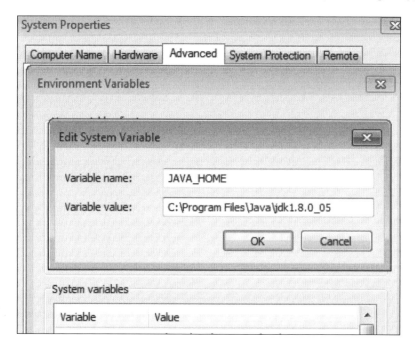

5. Test whether it's working by opening Command Prompt and entering java -version.

```
Command Prompt
Microsoft Windows [Version 6.1.7601]
Copyright (c) 2009 Microsoft Corporation.  All rights reserved.

C:\Users\jerome>java -version
java version "1.8.0_05"
Java(TM) SE Runtime Environment (build 1.8.0_05-b13)
Java HotSpot(TM) 64-Bit Server VM (build 25.5-b02, mixed mode)

C:\Users\jerome>_
```

Installing Maven

1. Download Maven from the Apache website http://maven.apache.org/ download.cgi. Choose the **Binary zip** file of the current stable version:

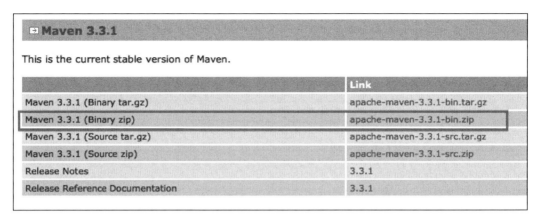

2. Uncompress the downloaded file.

3. Create a `Programs` folder in your user folder.

4. Move the extracted folder to it.

5. Navigate to **Control Panel | System and Security | System | Advanced system settings | Environment Variables...**.

6. Add a `MAVEN_HOME` system variable with the path to the Maven folder. For example, `C:\Users\jerome\Programs\apache-maven-3.2.1`.

7. Open the `Path` system variable.

8. Append `;%MAVEN_HOME%\bin` to it.

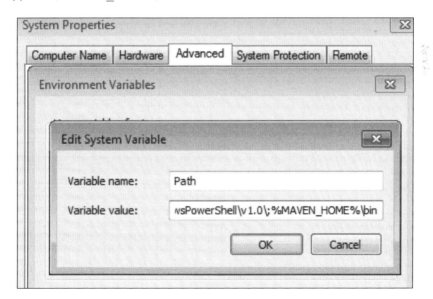

9. Test whether it's working by opening a Command Prompt and entering `mvn -v`.

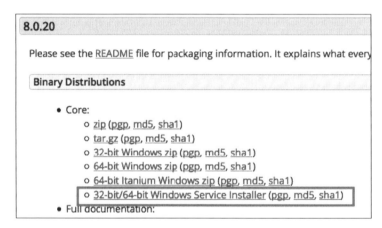

Installing Tomcat

1. Download Tomcat from the Apache website `http://tomcat.apache.org/download-80.cgi` and choose the **32-bit/64-bit Windows Service Installer** binary distribution.

> **8.0.20**
>
> Please see the README file for packaging information. It explains what every
>
> **Binary Distributions**
>
> - Core:
>   - zip (pgp, md5, sha1)
>   - tar.gz (pgp, md5, sha1)
>   - 32-bit Windows zip (pgp, md5, sha1)
>   - 64-bit Windows zip (pgp, md5, sha1)
>   - 64-bit Itanium Windows zip (pgp, md5, sha1)
>   - 32-bit/64-bit Windows Service Installer (pgp, md5, sha1)
> - Full documentation:

2. Launch and complete the installation.

3. Tomcat runs on the 8080 port by default. Go to `http://localhost:8080/` to check whether it's working.

Installing Eclipse

1. Download Eclipse from `http://www.eclipse.org/downloads/`. Choose the **Windows 64 Bit** version of **Eclipse IDE for Java EE Developers**.

 Eclipse IDE for Java EE Developers, 254 MB
Downloaded 372,729 Times

Tools for Java developers creating Java EE and Web applications, including a Java IDE, tools for Java EE, JPA, JSF, Mylyn... Windows 32 Bit
Windows 64 Bit

2. Uncompress the downloaded file.

3. Launch the `eclipse` program.

Creating a Spring web application

In this recipe, we will build a simple Spring web application with Eclipse. We will:

▶ Create a new Maven project

▶ Add Spring to it

▶ Add two Java classes to configure Spring

▶ Create a "Hello World" web page

In the next recipe, we will compile and run this web application.

How to do it...

In this section, we will create a Spring web application in Eclipse.

Creating a new Maven project in Eclipse

1. In Eclipse, in the **File** menu, select **New | Project...**.

2. Under **Maven**, select **Maven Project** and click on **Next >**.

3. Select the **Create a simple project (skip archetype selection)** checkbox and click on **Next >**.

4. For the **Group Id** field, enter `com.springcookbook`. For the **Artifact Id** field, enter `springwebapp`. For **Packaging**, select `war` and click on **Finish**.

Adding Spring to the project using Maven

Open Maven's `pom.xml` configuration file at the root of the project. Select the **pom.xml** tab to edit the XML source code directly. Under the `project` XML node, define the versions for Java and Spring. Also add the Servlet API, Spring Core, and Spring MVC dependencies:

```
<properties>
  <java.version>1.8</java.version>
  <spring.version>4.1.5.RELEASE</spring.version>
</properties>

<dependencies>
  <!-- Servlet API -->
  <dependency>
    <groupId>javax.servlet</groupId>
    <artifactId>javax.servlet-api</artifactId>
```

```
    <version>3.1.0</version>
    <scope>provided</scope>
  </dependency>

  <!-- Spring Core -->
  <dependency>
    <groupId>org.springframework</groupId>
    <artifactId>spring-context</artifactId>
    <version>${spring.version}</version>
  </dependency>

  <!-- Spring MVC -->
  <dependency>
    <groupId>org.springframework</groupId>
    <artifactId>spring-webmvc</artifactId>
    <version>${spring.version}</version>
  </dependency>
</dependencies>
```

Creating the configuration classes for Spring

1. Create the Java packages `com.springcookbook.config` and `com.springcookbook.controller`; in the left-hand side pane **Package Explorer**, right-click on the project folder and select **New | Package...**.

2. In the `com.springcookbook.config` package, create the `AppConfig` class. In the **Source** menu, select **Organize Imports** to add the needed import declarations:

    ```
    package com.springcookbook.config;
    @Configuration
    @EnableWebMvc
    @ComponentScan
    (basePackages = {"com.springcookbook.controller"})
    public class AppConfig {
    }
    ```

3. Still in the `com.springcookbook.config` package, create the `ServletInitializer` class. Add the needed import declarations similarly:

    ```
    package com.springcookbook.config;

    public class ServletInitializer extends
    AbstractAnnotationConfigDispatcherServletInitializer {
        @Override
        protected Class<?>[] getRootConfigClasses() {
            return new Class<?>[0];
        }
    ```

```
    @Override
    protected Class<?>[] getServletConfigClasses() {
        return new Class<?>[]{AppConfig.class};
    }

    @Override
    protected String[] getServletMappings() {
        return new String[]{"/"};
    }
}
```

Creating a "Hello World" web page

In the `com.springcookbook.controller` package, create the `HelloController` class and its `hi()` method:

```
@Controller
public class HelloController {
  @RequestMapping("hi")
  @ResponseBody
  public String hi() {
      return "Hello, world.";
  }
}
```

How it works...

This section will give more you details of what happened at every step.

Creating a new Maven project in Eclipse

The generated Maven project is a `pom.xml` configuration file along with a hierarchy of empty directories:

```
pom.xml
src
 |- main
    |- java
    |- resources
    |- webapp
 |- test
    |- java
    |- resources
```

Adding Spring to the project using Maven

The declared Maven libraries and their dependencies are automatically downloaded in the background by Eclipse. They are listed under **Maven Dependencies** in the left-hand side pane **Package Explorer**.

Tomcat provides the `Servlet API` dependency, but we still declared it because our code needs it to compile. Maven will not include it in the generated `.war` file because of the `<scope>provided</scope>` declaration.

Creating the configuration classes for Spring

`AppConfig` is a Spring configuration class. It is a standard Java class annotated with:

- ▶ `@Configuration`: This declares it as a Spring configuration class
- ▶ `@EnableWebMvc`: This enables Spring's ability to receive and process web requests
- ▶ `@ComponentScan(basePackages = {"com.springcookbook.controller"})`: This scans the `com.springcookbook.controller` package for Spring components

`ServletInitializer` is a configuration class for Spring's servlet; it replaces the standard `web.xml` file. It will be detected automatically by `SpringServletContainerInitializer`, which is automatically called by any Servlet 3. `ServletInitializer` extends the `AbstractAnnotationConfigDispatcherServletInitializer` abstract class and implements the required methods:

- ▶ `getServletMappings()`: This declares the servlet root URI.
- ▶ `getServletConfigClasses()`: This declares the Spring configuration classes. Here, we declared the `AppConfig` class that was previously defined.

Creating a "Hello World" web page

We created a controller class in the `com.springcookbook.controller` package, which we declared in `AppConfig`. When navigating to `http://localhost:8080/hi`, the `hi()` method will be called and **Hello, world.** will be displayed in the browser. This will be explained further in *Chapter 3, Using Controllers and Views*.

Running a Spring web application

In this recipe, we will use the Spring web application from the previous recipe. We will compile it with Maven and run it with Tomcat.

How to do it...

Here are the steps to compile and run a Spring web application:

1. In `pom.xml`, add this boilerplate code under the `project` XML node. It will allow Maven to generate `.war` files without requiring a `web.xml` file:

```
<build>
    <finalName>springwebapp</finalName>
  <plugins>
    <plugin>
      <groupId>org.apache.maven.plugins</groupId>
      <artifactId>maven-war-plugin</artifactId>
      <version>2.5</version>
      <configuration>
        <failOnMissingWebXml>false</failOnMissingWebXml>
      </configuration>
    </plugin>
  </plugins>
</build>
```

2. In Eclipse, in the left-hand side pane **Package Explorer**, select the `springwebapp` project folder. In the **Run** menu, select **Run** and choose **Maven install** or you can execute `mvn clean install` in a terminal at the root of the project folder. In both cases, a `target` folder will be generated with the `springwebapp.war` file in it.

3. Copy the `target/springwebapp.war` file to Tomcat's `webapps` folder.

4. Launch Tomcat.

5. In a web browser, go to `http://localhost:8080/springwebapp/hi` to check whether it's working.

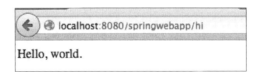

How it works...

In `pom.xml` the boilerplate code prevents Maven from throwing an error because there's no `web.xml` file. A `web.xml` file was required in Java web applications; however, since Servlet specification 3.0 (implemented in Tomcat 7 and higher versions), it's not required anymore.

There's more...

On Mac OS and Linux, you can create a symbolic link in Tomcat's `webapps` folder pointing to the `.war` file in your project folder. For example:

```
ln -s ~/eclipse_workspace/spring_webapp/target/springwebapp.war
~/bin/apache-tomcat/webapps/springwebapp.war
```

So, when the `.war` file is updated in your project folder, Tomcat will detect that it has been modified and will reload the application automatically.

Using Spring in a standard Java application

In this recipe, we will build a standard Java application (not a web application) using Spring. We will:

▶ Create a new Maven project

▶ Add Spring to it

▶ Add a class to configure Spring

▶ Add a `User` class

▶ Define a `User` singleton in the Spring configuration class

▶ Use the `User` singleton in the `main()` method

How to do it...

In this section, we will cover the steps to use Spring in a standard (not web) Java application.

Creating a new Maven project in Eclipse

1. In Eclipse, in the **File** menu, select **New | Project...**.

2. Under **Maven**, select **Maven Project** and click on **Next >**.

3. Select the **Create a simple project (skip archetype selection)** checkbox and click on **Next >**.

4. For the **Group Id** field, enter `com.springcookbook`. For the **Artifact Id** field, enter `springapp`. Click on **Finish**.

Adding Spring to the project using Maven

Open Maven's pom.xml configuration file at the root of the project. Select the **pom.xml** tab to edit the XML source code directly. Under the project XML node, define the Java and Spring versions and add the Spring Core dependency:

```
<properties>
  <java.version>1.8</java.version>
  <spring.version>4.1.5.RELEASE</spring.version>
</properties>

<dependencies>
  <!-- Spring Core -->
  <dependency>
    <groupId>org.springframework</groupId>
    <artifactId>spring-context</artifactId>
    <version>${spring.version}</version>
  </dependency>
</dependencies>
```

Creating a configuration class for Spring

1. Create the com.springcookbook.config Java package; in the left-hand side pane **Package Explorer**, right-click on the project and select **New | Package...**.

2. In the com.springcookbook.config package, create the AppConfig class. In the **Source** menu, select **Organize Imports** to add the needed import declarations:

```
@Configuration
public class AppConfig {
}
```

Creating the User class

Create a User Java class with two String fields:

```
public class User {
  private String name;
  private String skill;

  public String getName() {
    return name;
  }
  public void setName(String name) {
    this.name = name;
  }
  public String getSkill() {
    return skill;
```

```
  }
  public void setSkill(String skill) {
    this.skill = skill;
  }
}
```

Defining a User singleton in the Spring configuration class

In the `AppConfig` class, define a `User` bean:

```
@Bean
public User admin(){
  User u = new User();
  u.setName("Merlin");
  u.setSkill("Magic");
  return u;
}
```

Using the User singleton in the main() method

1. Create the `com.springcookbook.main` package with the `Main` class containing the `main()` method:

```
package com.springcookbook.main;
public class Main {
  public static void main(String[] args) {
}
}
```

2. In the `main()` method, retrieve the User singleton and print its properties:

```
AnnotationConfigApplicationContext springContext = new
AnnotationConfigApplicationContext(AppConfig.class);

User admin = (User) springContext.getBean("admin");

System.out.println("admin name: " + admin.getName());
System.out.println("admin skill: " + admin.getSkill());

springContext.close();
```

3. Test whether it's working; in the **Run** menu, select **Run**.

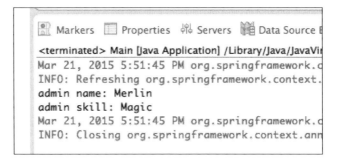

How it works...

We created a Java project to which we added Spring. We defined a `User` bean called `admin` (the bean name is by default the bean method name). Spring beans are explained in the next chapter.

In the `Main` class, we created a Spring context object from the `AppConfig` class and retrieved the `admin` bean from it. We used the bean and finally, closed the Spring context.

2
Defining Beans and Using Dependency Injection

In this chapter, we will cover the following recipes:

- ▶ Defining a bean explicitly with @Bean
- ▶ Defining a bean implicitly with @Component
- ▶ Using a bean via dependency injection with @Autowired
- ▶ Using a bean directly
- ▶ Listing all beans
- ▶ Using multiple configuration classes

Introduction

Beans are at the core of Spring. They are standard Java objects instantiated and managed by Spring.

Beans are mostly used to:

- ▶ Configure Spring in some way (database connection parameters, security, and so on)
- ▶ Avoid hardcoding dependencies using **dependency injection**, so that our classes remain self-contained and unit testable

In this chapter, you'll learn how to define beans and use them.

Defining a bean explicitly with @Bean

The simplest way to define a bean is to create, in a Spring configuration class, a method annotated with `@Bean` returning an object (the actual bean). Such beans are usually used to configure Spring in some way (database, security, view resolver, and so on). In this recipe, we'll define a bean that contains the connection details of a database.

How to do it...

In a Spring configuration class, add a `dataSource()` method annotated with `@Bean` and return a `Datasource` object. In this method, create a `DriverManagerDataSource` object initialized with the connection details of a database:

```
@Bean
public DataSource dataSource() {
        DriverManagerDataSource dataSource = new
DriverManagerDataSource();

        dataSource.setDriverClassName("com.mysql.jdbc.Driver");
        dataSource.setUrl("jdbc:mysql://localhost:3306/db1");
        dataSource.setUsername("root");
        dataSource.setPassword("123");

        return dataSource;
}
```

How it works...

At startup, because of `@Bean`, the `dataSource()` method is automatically executed and returns a `Datasource` object which is stored by Spring (in a Spring object called `ApplicationContext`). The bean name is `dataSource`, which is the same as its methods name. From this point, any call to `dataSource()` will return the same cached `DataSource` object; `dataSource()` won't actually be executed again. This is done using aspect-oriented programming; any call to `dataSource()` is intercepted by Spring, which directly returns the object instead of executing the method.

There's more...

To customize the bean name, use the name parameter:

```
@Bean(name="theSource")
public DataSource dataSource() {
...
```

To force `dataSource()` to be executed each time it's called (and return a different object each time), use the `@Scope` annotation with a `prototype` scope:

```
@Bean
@Scope(ConfigurableBeanFactory.SCOPE_PROTOTYPE)
public DataSource dataSource() {
...
```

It's possible to define beans using our own classes. For example, if we have a `UserService` class, we can define a `UserService` bean in a Spring configuration class:

```
@Bean
public UserService userService() {
        return new UserService();
}
```

However, it's usually simpler to let Spring generate this kind of beans automatically using a `@Component` annotation on the `UserService` class, as explained in the *Defining a bean implicitly with @Component* recipe.

Defining a bean implicitly with @Component

Beans don't have to be defined in a Spring configuration class. Spring will automatically generate a bean from any class annotated with `@Component`.

Getting ready

We will use the basic web application created in the *Creating a Spring web application* recipe in *Chapter 1, Creating a Spring Application*.

Create the `com.springcookbook.service` package and the following service class in it:

```
public class UserService {
  public int findNumberOfUsers() {
    return 10;
  }
}
```

How to do it...

Here are the steps to define a bean by adding `@Component` to an existing class:

1. In the Spring configuration file, in the `@ComponentScan` class annotation, add the `com.springcookbook.service` base package:

    ```
    @Configuration
    @EnableWebMvc
    ```

```
@ComponentScan(basePackages =
{"com.springcookbook.controller",
"com.springcookbook.service"})
public class AppConfig {
}
```

2. In the `UserService` class, add `@Component`:

```
@Component
public class UserService {
  public int findNumberOfUsers() {
    return 10;
  }
}
```

How it works...

At startup, the `com.springcookbook.service` package will be scanned by Spring. The `UserService` class is annotated with `@Component`, so a bean is automatically instantiated from it. The bean's name will be `userService` by default, based on the class name.

To specify a custom name, use the following code:

```
@Component('anAmazingUserService')
public class UserService {
```

There's more...

If the `UserService` bean requires some custom initialization, for example, based on the current environment, it's possible to define and initialize the bean explicitly as explained in the previous recipe, *Defining a bean explicitly with @Bean*.

`@Controller`, `@Service`, and `@Repository` are also component annotations; Spring will automatically instantiate a bean at startup from the classes annotated with them. It's not strictly necessary to use these component annotations, but they make the role of the component class clearer; `@Controller` is used for controller classes, `@Service` is used for service classes (so that's the one we would actually use for our `UserService` class), and `@Repository` is used for persistence classes. They also add minor extra functionality to the component classes. Refer to `http://docs.spring.io/spring-framework/docs/current/spring-framework-reference/html/beans.html#beans-stereotype-annotations`.

Using a bean via dependency injection with @Autowired

Spring configuration beans, such as the one in the *Defining a bean explicitly with @Bean* recipe are automatically discovered and used by Spring. To use a bean (any kind of bean) in one of your classes, add the bean as a field and annotate it with `@Autowired`. Spring will automatically initialize the field with the bean. In this recipe, we'll use an existing bean in a controller class.

Getting ready

We will use the code from the *Defining a bean implicitly with @Component* recipe, where we defined a `UserService` bean.

How to do it...

Here are the steps to use an existing bean in one of your classes:

1. In the controller class, add a `UserService` field annotated with `@Autowired`:

   ```
   @Autowired
   UserService userService;
   ```

2. In a controller method, use the `UserService` field:

   ```
   @RequestMapping("hi")
   @ResponseBody
   public String hi() {
       return "nb of users: " + userService.findNumberOfUsers();
   }
   ```

3. In a web browser, go to `http://localhost:8080/hi` to check whether it's working.

How it works...

When the controller class is instantiated, Spring automatically initializes the `@Autowired` field with the existing `UserService` bean. This is called dependency injection; the controller class simply declares its dependency, a `UserService` field. It's Spring that initializes the field by injecting a `UserService` object into it.

If Spring is not able to find an existing bean for that dependency, an exception is thrown.

There's more...

It's possible to set the name of the bean to be used:

```
@Autowired("myUserService")
UserService userService;
```

Dependency injection is useful when interfaces are used. For example, we could replace our `UserService` class by a `UserService` interface and its implementation `UserServiceImpl`. Everything would work the same, except that it's now simple to swap `UserServiceImpl` for another class, for example, for unit testing purposes.

Using a bean directly

It's possible to get a bean directly from Spring instead of using dependency injection by making Spring's `ApplicationContext`, which contains all the beans, a dependency of your class. In this recipe, we'll inject an existing bean into a controller class.

Getting ready

We will use the code from the *Defining a bean implicitly with @Component* recipe, where we defined a `UserService` bean.

How to do it...

Here are the steps to get and use a bean directly:

1. In the controller class, add an `ApplicationContext` field annotated with `@Autowired`:

   ```
   @Autowired
   private ApplicationContext applicationContext;
   ```

2. In a controller method, use the `ApplicationContext` object and its `getBean()` method to retrieve the `UserService` bean:

   ```
   UserService userService =
   (UserService)applicationContext.getBean("userService");
   ```

How it works...

When the controller class is instantiated, Spring automatically initializes the `@Autowired` field with its `ApplicationContext` object. The `ApplicationContext` object references all Spring beans, so we can get a bean directly using its name.

There's more...

It's possible to get a bean by its class, without knowing its name.

```
applicationContext.getBean(UserService.class);
```

Listing all beans

It can be useful, especially for debugging purposes, to list all the beans at a given moment.

Getting ready

We will use the code from the *Defining a bean implicitly with @Component* recipe, where we defined a UserService bean.

How to do it...

Here are the steps to retrieve the names of the beans currently in Spring's ApplicationContext object:

1. In your class, add an ApplicationContext field annotated with @Autowired:

    ```
    @Autowired
    private ApplicationContext applicationContext;
    ```

2. In a method of that class, use ApplicationContext and its getBeanDefinitionNames() method to get the list of bean names:

    ```
    String[] beans =
    applicationContext.getBeanDefinitionNames();
    for (String bean : beans) {
      System.out.println(bean);
    }
    ```

How it works...

When the controller class is instantiated, Spring automatically initializes the @Autowired field with its ApplicationContext object. The ApplicationContext object references all Spring beans, so we can get a list of all the beans that are using it.

There's more...

To retrieve the bean itself from its name, use the getBean() method:

```
applicationContext.getBean("aBeanName");
```

Using multiple configuration classes

A Spring configuration class can get quite long with many bean definitions. At this point, it can be convenient to break it into multiple classes.

Getting ready

We will use the code from the *Defining a bean explicitly with @Bean* recipe.

How to do it...

Here's how to add a second configuration class:

1. Create a new configuration class, for example, `DatabaseConfig` in the `com.springcookbook.config` package:

    ```
    @Configuration
    public class DatabaseConfig {
        ...
    ```

2. In the `ServletInitializer` class, add the `DatabaseConfig` class in the `getServletConfigClasses()` method:

    ```
    @Override
    protected Class<?>[] getServletConfigClasses() {
        return new Class<?>[]{AppConfig.class,
    DatabaseConfig.class};
    }
    ```

3. Move the `Datasource` bean from the `AppConfig` class to `DatabaseConfig`.

There's more...

If you are using a Spring application without a `ServletInitializer` class, you can include other configuration classes from your primary configuration class:

```
@Configuration
@Import({ DatabaseConfig.class, SecurityConfig.class })
public class AppConfig {
    ...
}
```

3
Using Controllers and Views

In this chapter, we will cover the following recipes:

- ▸ Associating a route to a controller method
- ▸ Using a JSP view
- ▸ Passing attributes from a controller to a JSP view
- ▸ Using dynamic route parameters in a controller method
- ▸ Using a common prefix for the routes of a controller
- ▸ Using a page template with Tiles
- ▸ Executing some code before and after controllers using interceptors
- ▸ Building multilingual pages

Introduction

A Spring web application uses a **MVC (Model-View-Controller)** architecture to process HTTP requests, as shown in the following image:

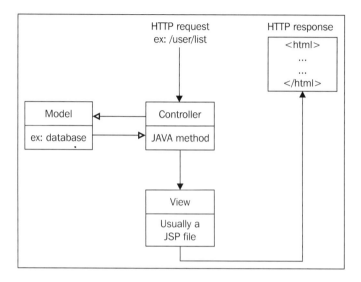

An HTTP request, identified by a route (for example, `/user/list`), executes a controller method. A view, usually a JSP file, is rendered afterwards and the resulting HTML is sent back as a response.

In this chapter, we will start by creating a controller and view. Then, you'll learn how to retrieve URL parameters from a controller method. We'll cover two standard ways to reduce code repetition with page templates and URL prefixes. We will finish with more advanced topics related to controllers and views: interceptors and internationalization.

The recipes in this chapter will work with a project similar to the one in the *Creating a Spring web application* recipe in *Chapter 1, Creating a Spring Application*, with a Spring configuration class annotated with `@EnableWebMvc` and scanning a Java package dedicated to controller classes:

```
@Configuration
@EnableWebMvc
@ComponentScan(basePackages = {"com.springcookbook.controller"})
public class AppConfig {
}
```

This is the project structure:

Associating a route to a controller method

In this recipe, you will learn how to define a controller method to be executed for a given route.

How to do it...

Here are the steps for creating a controller method for a given route:

1. Create a controller class in your controller package (for example, `com.springcookbook.controller`). This is a normal Java class annotated with `@Controller`:

```
@Controller
public class UserController {
    ...
}
```

2. Add a controller method. This is a standard Java method annotated with `@RequestMapping`, which takes the route as a parameter:

```
@RequestMapping("/user/list")
public void userList() {
    ...
}
```

How it works...

A request with the `/user/list` route will execute the `userList()` method.

Using a JSP view

In this recipe, you'll learn how to render and return a JSP view after the execution of a controller method.

How to do it...

Here are the steps to create a JSP view:

1. Add the Maven dependency for JSTL in `pom.xml`:

```
<dependency>
  <groupId>javax.servlet</groupId>
  <artifactId>jstl</artifactId>
  <version>1.2</version>
</dependency>
```

2. Add a JSP view resolver to the Spring configuration class:

```
@Bean
public ViewResolver jspViewResolver(){
    InternalResourceViewResolver resolver = new
InternalResourceViewResolver();
    resolver.setViewClass(JstlView.class);
    resolver.setPrefix("/WEB-INF/jsp/");
    resolver.setSuffix(".jsp");
    return resolver;
}
```

3. Create a controller method:

```
@RequestMapping("/user/list")
public void userList() {
   ...
}
```

4. Create the `/WEB-INF/jsp/user/list.jsp` JSP:

```
<html>
<body>
   There are many users.
</body>
</html>
```

How it works...

The controller method path is `/user/list`. Using the JSP view resolver, Spring will find and render the corresponding `/WEB-INF/jsp/user/list.jsp` JSP.

If the path had been `/user_list`, the corresponding JSP would have been `/WEB-INF/jsp/user_list.jsp`.

This is the current project structure:

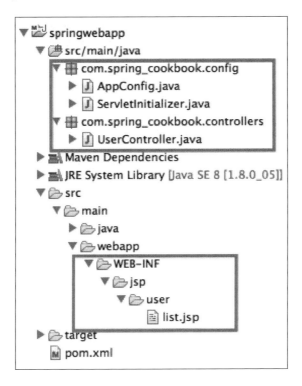

There's more...

It's possible to explicitly return a `String` object from the controller method, which Spring will use to find the JSP. In this example, `/WEB-INF/jsp/my_friends.jsp` will be used:

```
@RequestMapping("/user/list")
public String userList() {
    return "my_friends";
}
```

For more information about what can be done in a JSP file, refer to `http://www.tutorialspoint.com/jsp/jsp_standard_tag_library.htm`.

Thymeleaf, FreeMarker, and Velocity are popular view frameworks that provide an alternative to JSPs. FreeMarker and Velocity are supported by Spring by default. Thymeleaf provides its own view resolver.

Passing attributes from a controller to a JSP view

In this recipe, you'll learn how to set attributes in a controller method and use them in a JSP view.

How to do it...

Here are the steps to pass data from a controller to a view:

1. Add a `Model` argument to the controller method:

    ```
    @RequestMapping("/user/list")
    public void userList(Model model) {
    ...
    ```

2. In the controller method, add attributes to the `Model` object:

    ```
    model.addAttribute("nbUsers", 13);
    ```

3. Use the attributes in the JSP file:

    ```
    <p>There are ${nbUsers} users</p>
    ```

How it works...

The `nbUsers` variable is set to `13` in the controller. In the JSP file, the `${nbUsers}` **EL (Expression Language)** element will be rendered to `13`, so that the following HTML will be returned:

```
<p>There are 13 users</p>
```

Using dynamic route parameters in a controller method

Now we will define dynamic segments for a route and use them in the associated controller method. For example, we want the `/user/5/name` and `/user/6/email` routes to execute the same controller method with different arguments: `showUserField(5, "name")` and `showUserField(6, "email")`, respectively.

How to do it...

Use { } to enclose the dynamic route segments and `@PathVariable` to annotate the corresponding controller method arguments:

```
@RequestMapping("/user/{id}/{field}")
public void showUserField(@PathVariable("id") Long userId,
@PathVariable("field") String field) {

...
}
```

How it works...

A request for the `/user/5/email` route will execute the `showUserField(5,"email")` method. `@PathVariable("id") Long userId` casts the id route parameter to the `userId` method argument. Similarly, the `field` route parameter is passed as `String` to `showUserField()`.

An incorrect route such as `/user/test/email` (it's incorrect because the `test` substring cannot be converted to a `Long` object) will trigger a 400 server error with the message **The request sent by the client was syntactically incorrect.**

Using a common prefix for the routes of a controller

In this recipe, we will define in one place a route prefix shared by all the routes of a controller. We will start the routes of the `UserController` controller with `/user`.

How to do it...

Here are the steps to set a route prefix:

1. Add `@RequestMapping` with the common route prefix to the controller class:

```
@Controller
@RequestMapping("/user")
public class UserController {

...
}
```

2. Add `@RequestMapping` with the remainder of the route to the controller methods:

```
@RequestMapping("/list")
public void userList() {
    ...
}

@RequestMapping("/add")
public void addUser() {
    ...
}
```

How it works...

A request for the `/user/add` route will execute the `addUser()` method. A request for the `/user/list` route will execute the `userList()` method.

Using a page template with Tiles

With a page template, avoid repeating the common elements of the pages (HTML head, header, footer, navigation, and so on) in every JSP.

How to do it...

Here are the steps to use Tiles:

1. Add the Tiles Maven dependencies in `pom.xml`:

```
<dependency>
    <groupId>org.apache.tiles</groupId>
    <artifactId>tiles-servlet</artifactId>
    <version>3.0.5</version>
</dependency>

<dependency>
    <groupId>org.apache.tiles</groupId>
    <artifactId>tiles-jsp</artifactId>
    <version>3.0.5</version>
</dependency>
```

2. In the Spring configuration class, remove the JSP view resolver (if it's there).

3. Declare Tiles in the Spring configuration class:

```java
// declare Tiles configuration file
@Bean
public TilesConfigurer tilesConfigurer() {
  TilesConfigurer tilesConfigurer = new TilesConfigurer();
  final String[] definitions = { "/WEB-INF/tiles.xml" };
    tilesConfigurer.setDefinitions(definitions);
  return tilesConfigurer;
}

// declare Tiles as a view resolver
@Bean
public ViewResolver tilesViewResolver() {
  TilesViewResolver resolver = new TilesViewResolver();
  return resolver;
}
```

4. Create the `/WEB-INF/tiles.xml` Tiles configuration file:

```xml
<tiles-definitions>

    <definition name="template"
template="/WEB-INF/jsp/templates/template.jsp" />

    <definition name="*" extends="template">
        <put-attribute name="body"
value="/WEB-INF/jsp/{1}.jsp" />
    </definition>

</tiles-definitions>
```

5. Create the `/WEB-INF/jsp/templates/template.jsp` page template:

```jsp
<!DOCTYPE HTML>
<%@ taglib prefix="tiles"
uri="http://tiles.apache.org/tags-tiles" %>

<html>
<head>
    <meta charset="utf-8">
</head>
<body>
    <h1>Spring Cookbook</h1>

    <tiles:insertAttribute name="body" />
```

```
    </body>
    </html>
```

6. In the controller methods, return the base name of a standard JSP file. For example, for `/jsp/home.jsp`:

```
    ...
    return "home";
```

How it works...

When the Spring configuration is loaded, Tiles is initialized using the declared `tiles.xml` configuration file.

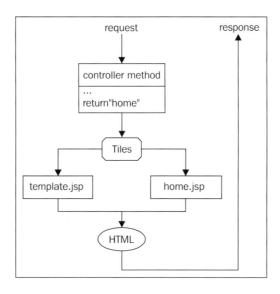

When a request arrives, the controller method is executed and returns the `"home"` String, which matches the definition named `"*"` in `tiles.xml`. This definition will use the `template` definition and pass the `body` variable to it with the `/WEB-INF/jsp/home.jsp` value. In `template.jsp`, the `tiles:insertAttribute` tag will be replaced by the contents of `home.jsp`.

To summarize, the `home.jsp` file is integrated with `template.jsp` and the resulting HTML is sent as a response.

In `template.php`, make sure to include the following to be able to use Tiles tags such as `<tiles:insertAttribute>`:

```
    <%@ taglib prefix="tiles" uri="http://tiles.apache.org/tags-tiles"
    %>
```

There's more...

Tiles can be used when JSP files are in subfolders and support multiple page templates. It's also possible to define repeated text in one place.

Organizing the JSP with subfolders

As the number of JSP files grows, you can maintain them by grouping them according to sections, using subfolders:

```
/jsp
 |- /user
 |    |- list.jsp
 |    |- add.jsp
 |- /article
 |    |- list.jsp
 |    |- add.jsp
 |- home.jsp
```

In the controller method, return the folder with the `jsp` base name, for example, `user/list`.

In `tiles.xml`, add the definition:

```
<definition name="*/*" extends="template">
    <put-attribute name="body" value="/WEB-INF/jsp/{1}/{2}.jsp" />
</definition>
```

Using multiple page templates

To handle multiple templates, define a prefix for each template in `tiles.xml`. For example, we defined below a main template with the `main_` prefix using the `template1.jsp` JSP and a secondary template with the `secondary_` prefix using the `template2.jsp` JSP:

```
    <definition name="template1"
template="/WEB-INF/templates/template1.jsp" />
    <definition name="template2"
template="/WEB-INF/templates/template2.jsp" />

    <definition name="main_*" extends="template1">
        <put-attribute name="body" value="/WEB-INF/jsp/{1}.jsp" />
    </definition>

    <definition name="secondary_*" extends="template2">
        <put-attribute name="body" value="/WEB-INF/jsp/{1}.jsp" />
    </definition>
```

In the controller method, for `home.jsp`, return `"main_home"` to use `template1` or `"secondary_home"` to use `template2`.

Defining page titles only once using a text attribute

A title usually needs to appear twice in an HTML page: once in the `<title>` tag of the page `<head>` section and once in a `<h1>` tag of the page `<body>` section. Using Tiles, you can define it only once in an external `.properties` file:

1. In `tiles.xml`, add a title attribute to the template definition:

```
<definition name="*" extends="template">
  <put-attribute name="title" value="{1}.title" />
...
```

2. In `template.jsp`, get the title and use it:

```
<!DOCTYPE HTML>
<%@ taglib prefix="spring"
uri="http://www.springframework.org/tags" %>
<%@ taglib prefix="tiles"
uri="http://tiles.apache.org/tags-tiles" %>

<c:set var="titleKey">
  <tiles:getAsString name="title" />
</c:set>

<html>
<head>
   <title><spring:message code="${titleKey}" />/title>
</head>
<body>
  <h1><spring:message code="${titleKey}" /></h1>
   ...
```

3. Create the `src/main/resources/messages.properties` file:

```
home.title=Home
```

To learn more about Tiles, go to `https://tiles.apache.org/framework/tutorial/`.

Executing some code before and after controllers using interceptors

In this recipe, you'll learn how, with interceptors, we can execute some code across all controllers at different moments of a request workflow with the `preHandle()`, `postHandle()`, and `afterCompletion()` hooks:

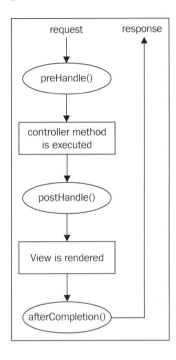

Interceptors are used for authentication, logging, and profiling (among others).

How to do it...

Here are the steps to create and register an interceptor:

1. Create a class extending `HandlerInterceptorAdapter`:

   ```
   public class PerformanceInterceptor extends
   HandlerInterceptorAdapter {
   ```

2. Override the methods you want to use:

   ```
   @Override
   public boolean preHandle(HttpServletRequest request,
       HttpServletResponse response, Object handler) throws
   Exception {
   ```

```
    ...
  return true;
}


@Override
public void postHandle(HttpServletRequest request,
    HttpServletResponse response, Object handler,
    ModelAndView modelAndView) throws Exception {
  ...
}


@Override
public void afterCompletion(HttpServletRequest request,
    HttpServletResponse response, Object handler, Exception
ex)
    throws Exception {
  ...
}
```

 Note that if `preHandle()` returns `false`, the request workflow will be stopped and the controller method won't be called.

3. Make the Spring configuration class extend `WebMvcConfigurerAdapter` and annotate it with `@EnableWebMvc`:

```
@Configuration
@EnableWebMvc
public class AppConfig extends WebMvcConfigurerAdapter{
...
```

4. In the Spring configuration class, declare the interceptor as a bean and register it with the `addInterceptors()` method:

```
@Bean
public HandlerInterceptor performanceInterceptor() {
  PerformanceInterceptor interceptor;
  interceptor = new PerformanceInterceptor();
  return interceptor;
}


@Override
public void addInterceptors(InterceptorRegistry registry) {
  registry.addInterceptor(performanceInterceptor());
}
```

How it works...

The interceptor methods are executed at the corresponding moments of the request workflow.

There's more...

To restrict the interceptor to specific URLs, add path patterns to the interceptor registration:

```
@Override
public void addInterceptors(InterceptorRegistry registry) {
  registry.addInterceptor(performanceInterceptor())
.addPathPatterns("/home", "/user/*");
}
```

In this example, the interceptor methods will be executed for `/home`, `/user/list`, and `/user/add` but not for `/contact`.

Building multilingual pages

Next we will learn how to create a multilingual page (in English and French) using only one JSP, and display it in English by default, with a link to switch to French. We will then store the text outside the JSP, in both languages, in separate `.properties` files.

How to do it...

Here are the steps to build a bilingual JSP view:

1. Create the JSP:

```
<%@ taglib prefix="spring"
uri="http://www.springframework.org/tags" %>

<html>
<body>
  <h1><spring:message code="home.title" /></h1>
  <p><spring:message code="home.intro" /></p>

  <p>
    <a href="?lang=en">English</a> |
    <a href="?lang=fr">French</a>
  </p>
</body>
</html>
```

2. Create the English `.properties` file `src/main/resources/messages.properties`:

```
home.title=Home
home.intro=This is a magnificent home page, isn't it?
```

3. Create the French `.properties` file `src/main/resources/messages_fr.properties`:

```
home.title=Accueil
home.intro=Splendide page d'accueil, non ?
```

4. In Spring configuration, declare the `.properties` files:

```
@Bean
public MessageSource messageSource() {
  ReloadableResourceBundleMessageSource messageSource = new
ReloadableResourceBundleMessageSource();
  messageSource.setBasename("classpath:/messages");
  messageSource.setUseCodeAsDefaultMessage(true);
  return messageSource;
}
```

5. Make sure that the Spring configuration class extends `WebMvcConfigurerAdapter` and is annotated with `@EnableWebMvc`:

```
@Configuration
@EnableWebMvc
public class AppConfig extends WebMvcConfigurerAdapter{
...
```

6. Define a `LocaleChangeInterceptor` interceptor to allow the current language to be changed with a `lang` URL parameter. Register the interceptor:

```
@Bean
public HandlerInterceptor localeChangeInterceptor() {
  LocaleChangeInterceptor interceptor = new
LocaleChangeInterceptor();
  interceptor.setParamName("lang");
  return interceptor;
}

@Override
public void addInterceptors(InterceptorRegistry registry) {
  registry.addInterceptor(localeChangeInterceptor());
}
```

7. Store the user language selection in a cookie and declare the default language:

```
@Bean
public LocaleResolver localeResolver() {
  CookieLocaleResolver localeResolver = new
CookieLocaleResolver();
  localeResolver.setDefaultLocale(new Locale("en"));
  return localeResolver;
}
```

How it works...

The following steps describe how the preceding code works:

1. When a request comes in, Spring first checks whether it has a cookie value containing a language. If the answer is yes, it uses it as the current language; otherwise, it uses the default language. This behavior comes from the declaration of `CookieLocaleResolver` as the locale resolver.

2. The `LocaleChangeInterceptor` then checks whether there's a `lang` parameter in the URL. If the answer is yes, it uses it as the current language (instead of the default or cookie language).

3. When `home.jsp` is rendered, its text is fetched from the `.properties` file corresponding to the current language. If no text is found for a given message key, the key itself is displayed. This behavior comes from `messageSource.setUseCodeAsD efaultMessage(true)`.

There's more...

You may need to retrieve the current language name from a controller method. You may also need to have the page language in the URL instead of in a cookie.

Getting the current language

To retrieve the current language from a controller or an interceptor, use the following code:

```
Locale locale = LocaleContextHolder.getLocale();
String lang = locale.getLanguage(); // fr
String language = locale.getDisplayLanguage(); // French
String language2 = locale.getDisplayLanguage(locale); // français
```

Using the language in the URL

Spring does not provide a convenient way to handle the language in the URL (for example, `/en/user/list`). Instead, it has to be done manually:

1. Use an interceptor to retrieve the language from the URL and override the current language.

2. Prefix the controller method mappings with the supported languages (so that Spring can retrieve it from the route with the language):

```
@Controller
@RequestMapping("{en|fr}/user/*")
public class UserController {
  @RequestMapping("list")
  public String userList(Model model) {
    ...
  }
}.
```

3. When generating an internal link, prefix it with the current language, assuming that `$lang` contains the current language:

```
<spring:url value="/${lang}/home" var="home" />
<a href="${home}">Home</a>
```

4

Querying a Database

In this chapter, we will cover the following recipes:

- Connecting to a database
- Creating a DAO class
- Calling a DAO method from a controller class
- Saving an object
- Retrieving an object
- Retrieving a list of objects
- Retrieving a list of objects with their dependencies
- Updating an object
- Deleting an object
- Finding the number of results for an SQL query
- Saving a list of objects at once
- Reverting incomplete database modifications using transactions
- Using Hibernate for powerful object persistence and querying

Introduction

JDBC (Java Database Connectivity) and **Hibernate** are the two most commonly used technologies to query a database from a Spring application.

For small projects and simple data models, JDBC is straightforward; you write your SQL queries yourself and Spring provides helpers to convert the query results into objects.

For complex data models, with several relationships between classes, Hibernate is easier; you deal with a standard Java framework (still using JDBC behind the scenes) that will generate the SQL queries for you.

This chapter focuses on JDBC because Spring doesn't change the normal way of using Hibernate. The integration of Hibernate with Spring, however, is covered in the *Using Hibernate for powerful object persistence and querying* recipe.

Connecting to a database

In this recipe, we will connect to a MySQL or PostgreSQL database from a Spring application. To connect to another database system, go to `http://www.oxygenxml.com/database_drivers.html` to find the relevant dependencies, driver class, and URL type.

Getting ready

You need a MySQL or PostgreSQL database up and running.

How to do it...

Here are the steps to connect from a Spring application to an existing database:

1. Add the Maven dependency for Spring JDBC in `pom.xml`:

```
<dependency>
  <groupId>org.springframework</groupId>
  <artifactId>spring-jdbc</artifactId>
  <version>4.1.6.RELEASE</version>
</dependency>
```

2. If you're using MySQL, add its Maven dependency in `pom.xml`:

```
<dependency>
  <groupId>mysql</groupId>
  <artifactId>mysql-connector-java</artifactId>
  <version>5.1.35</version>
</dependency>
```

3. If you're using PostgreSQL, add its Maven dependency in `pom.xml`:

```
<dependency>
  <groupId>postgresql</groupId>
  <artifactId>postgresql</artifactId>
  <version>9.1-901-1.jdbc4</version>
</dependency>
```

In the Spring configuration, add a `DataSource` bean with the database connection details.

1. If you're using MySQL:

```
@Bean
public DataSource dataSource() {
        DriverManagerDataSource dataSource = new
DriverManagerDataSource();

        dataSource.setDriverClassName("com.mysql.jdbc.Driver");
        dataSource.setUrl("jdbc:mysql://localhost:3306/db1");
        dataSource.setUsername("user1");
        dataSource.setPassword("pass1");

        return dataSource;
}
```

2. If you're using PostgreSQL:

```
@Bean
public DataSource dataSource() {
    DriverManagerDataSource dataSource = new
DriverManagerDataSource();

    dataSource.setDriverClassName("org.postgresql.Driver");
    dataSource.setUrl("jdbc:postgresql://localhost:5432/db1");
    dataSource.setUsername("user1");
    dataSource.setPassword("pass1");

    return dataSource;
}
```

3. In the Spring configuration, add a `JdbcTemplate` bean, taking `DataSource` as an argument:

```
@Bean
public JdbcTemplate jdbcTemplate(DataSource dataSource) {
  return new JdbcTemplate(dataSource);
}
```

How it works...

A connection (a `Datasource` object) to a database named `db1` on the `3306` port (MySQL) or the `5432` port (PostgreSQL) using the `user1` user is created.

The `JdbcTemplate` bean is a Spring object that provides convenient methods to query a database using JDBC. It uses the previously defined `DataSource` bean. We will use the `JdbcTemplate` bean from our DAO classes.

Creating a DAO class

In this recipe, we will create a **DAO** (**data access object**) class. A DAO class provides methods to save and retrieve objects from the database. It can be used from a controller, for example:

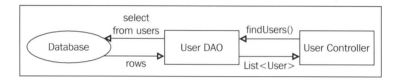

The controller calls the `findUsers()` method from `UserDAO`, which takes care of getting the results from the database (using the `JdbcTemplate` bean defined in the previous recipe).

How to do it...

Here are the steps to create a DAO class:

1. Create a class annotated with `@Repository`:

   ```
   @Repository
   public class UserDAO {
   ```

2. Add an autowired `JdbcTemplate` field to it:

   ```
   @Autowired
   private JdbcTemplate jdbcTemplate;
   ```

How it works...

`@Repository` allows the `UserDAO` class to be automatically discovered and instantiated as a bean.

The `JdbcTemplate` field will be initialized automatically by Spring via dependency injection with the `JdbcTemplate` bean defined in the previous recipe.

Calling a DAO method from a controller class

In this recipe, we'll see how to call a DAO method from a controller class.

Getting ready

We will use the DAO class defined in the previous recipe and pretend that it has an `add(User)` method. In the following recipes, we will write actual DAO methods.

How to do it...

Here are the steps to use a DAO method from a controller class:

1. In your controller class, add the DAO as an `@Autowired` field:

    ```
    @Controller
    public class UserController {
        @Autowired
        private UserDAO userDAO;
    ```

2. Use the DAO in any controller method:

    ```
    userDAO.add(user);
    ```

How it works...

Because of `@Autowired`, the `userDAO` field will be automatically initialized by Spring using dependency injection.

Saving an object

In this recipe, we will create a DAO method to save an object in the database; a row will be added to the corresponding database table, for example:

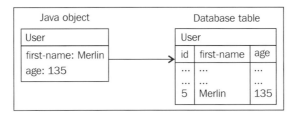

Getting ready

You need to have a model class, for example:

```
public class User {
  private Long id;
  private String firstName;
  private Integer age;
```

You need to have a matching database table, for example:

```
CREATE TABLE `user` (
  `id` int(11) AUTO_INCREMENT,
  `first_name` text,
  `age` int(11),
  PRIMARY KEY (`id`)
)
```

You need to have a DAO class with a JdbcTemplate attribute (Refer to the *Creating a DAO class* recipe)

How to do it...

Define an SQL insert query with question marks as placeholders for the actual row values. Use the update() method to execute the query using the actual values from the object:

```
public void add(User user) {
  String sql = "insert into user (first_name, age) values (?, ?)";
  jdbcTemplate.update(sql, user.getFirstName(), user.getAge());
}
```

How it works...

The jdbcTemplate object takes care of the JDBC boilerplate code; opening and closing a connection to the database and handling the exceptions. The update() method takes the SQL query and the actual values that will replace the question marks in the SQL query.

Retrieving an object

In this recipe, we create a DAO method to retrieve a database row, which we will use to create an object.

How to do it...

Use an SQL select query and create an object from the result using `RowMapper`:

1. In the DAO class, add an inline class implementing `RowMapper`. This class defines how to generate a `User` object from a database row:

```
private class UserMapper implements RowMapper<User> {
  public User mapRow(ResultSet row, int rowNum) throws
SQLException {
    User user = new User();

    user.setId(row.getLong("id"));
    user.setFirstName(row.getString("first_name"));
    user.setAge(row.getInt("age"));

    return user;
  }
}
```

2. Add a DAO method which will perform an SQL `select` query and use a `UserMapper` object to generate a `User` object:

```
public User findById(Long id) {
  String sql = "select * from user where id=?";
  User user = jdbcTemplate.queryForObject(sql, new
Object[]{id}, new UserMapper());
  return user;
}
```

How it works...

The `queryForObject()` method uses the `UserMapper` object to generate a `User` object from the resulting database row.

In this example, we retrieve a user from its ID, which is the second argument of `queryForObject()`, as an element of an array.

If the database column names match the names of the object attributes, there's no need to define a custom RowMapper interface, just use a ParameterizedBeanPropertyRowMapper class:

```
public User findById(Long id) {
  String sql = "select * from user where id=?";
  User user = jdbcTemplate.queryForObject(sql, new Object[]{id},
ParameterizedBeanPropertyRowMapper.newInstance(User.class));
  return user;
}
```

Retrieving a list of objects

In this recipe, we will add a DAO method to retrieve database rows and create a list of objects from them.

How to do it...

Perform an SQL select query and generate a list of objects from the result using RowMapper:

```
public List<User> findAll() {
  String sql = "select * from user";
  List<User> userList = jdbcTemplate.query(sql,
ParameterizedBeanPropertyRowMapper.newInstance(User.class));
  return userList;
}
```

How it works...

The query() method uses RowMapper to generate objects from the returned database rows.

We used a ParameterizedBeanPropertyRowMapper class assuming that the database table columns match the object attributes; however, as in the previous recipe, a custom RowMapper interface can be used.

Retrieving a list of objects with their dependencies

In this recipe, we will add a DAO method to generate, from an SQL query joining several tables, a list of objects with their dependencies. We will retrieve a list of `User` objects along with their `Post` objects (blog posts written by these users).

Getting ready

You need to have model classes related to each other. In this example, a user has many posts:

```java
public class User {
  private Long id;
  private String firstName;
  private Integer age;
  private LinkedList<Post> posts = new LinkedList<Post>();

public class Post {
  private long id;
  private String title;
  private Date date;
  private User user;
```

You need to have corresponding database tables, for example:

```sql
CREATE TABLE `user` (
  `id` int(11) AUTO_INCREMENT,
  `first_name` text,
  `age` int(11),
  PRIMARY KEY (`id`)
)

CREATE TABLE `post` (
  `id` int(11) AUTO_INCREMENT,
  `title` text,
  `date` datetime,
  `user_id` int(11),
  PRIMARY KEY (`id`),
  CONSTRAINT `user_id` FOREIGN KEY (`id`) REFERENCES `user` (`id`)
)
```

How to do it...

Use an SQL `select` query and generate a list of objects from the result using a class implementing `ResultSetExtractor`, which goes through the whole list of rows before returning the list of objects:

1. Add a DAO method performing an SQL `select` statement with `left join` and using `ResultSetExtractor` to generate a list of objects:

```
public List<User> findAll() {
  String sql = "select u.id, u.first_name, u.age,
p.id as p_id, p.title as p_title,
p.date as p_date from user u left join post p on
p.user_id = u.id order by u.id asc, p.date desc";
  return jdbcTemplate.query(sql, new UserWithPosts());
}
```

2. Add an inline class implementing `ResultSetExtractor`:

```
private class UserWithPosts implements
ResultSetExtractor<List<User>> {

  public List<User> extractData(ResultSet rs) throws
SQLException,
      DataAccessException {

    Map<Long, User> userMap = new ConcurrentHashMap<Long,
User>();
    User u = null;
    while (rs.next()) {
      // user already in map?
      Long id = rs.getLong("id");
      u = userMap.get(id);

      // if not, add it
      if(u == null) {
        u = new User();
        u.setId(id);
        u.setFirstName(rs.getString("first_name"));
        u.setAge(rs.getInt("age"));
        userMap.put(id, u);
      }

      // create post if there's one
      Long postId = rs.getLong("p_id");
```

```
        if (postId > 0) {
          System.out.println("add post id=" + postId);
          Post p = new Post();
          p.setId(postId);
          p.setTitle(rs.getString("p_title"));
          p.setDate(rs.getDate("p_date"));
          p.setUser(u);
          u.getPosts().add(p);
        }
      }

      return new LinkedList<User>(userMap.values());
    }
  }
}
```

How it works...

Because of `left join`, we obtain a list of rows from the database with sometimes the same user, but representing different posts. Each row cannot be processed independently or we would end up creating the same user multiple times. So, we use `ResultSetExtractor`, which allows us to go through the list of rows.

We use a map of `User` objects to track whether the `User` for the current row has already been created.

In the SQL query, we explicitly listed the column names to ensure that they will have different names in the resulting rows. Otherwise, `Post id` could be confused with `User id`, for example.

Updating an object

In this recipe, we will add a DAO method to update an existing row in the database with an object's fields.

How to do it...

Use an SQL `update` query and execute it using the `update()` method:

```
public void update(User user) {
  String sql = "update user set first_name=?, age=? where id=?";
  jdbcTemplate.update(sql, user.getFirstName(), user.getAge(),
user.getId());
}
```

There's more...

It's convenient to also have a `save()` method that will create the database row if it doesn't exist:

```java
public void save(User user) {
  if (user.getId() == null) {
    add(user);
  }
  else {
    update(user);
  }
}
```

Deleting an object

In this recipe, we will add a DAO method to delete an existing row from the database.

How to do it...

Use an SQL `delete` query and execute it using the `update()` method:

```java
public void delete(User user) {
  String sql = "delete from user where id=?";
  getJdbcTemplate().update(sql, user.getId());
}
```

Finding the number of results for an SQL query

In this recipe, we will add a DAO method to quickly get the number of results for an SQL query without actually loading the rows in the memory.

How to do it...

Use an SQL `count(*)` function and get the value directly using the `queryForObject()` method with a second argument specifying `Long` as the returned type:

```java
public long countMinorUsers() {
  String sql = "select count(*) from age < 18";
  return jdbcTemplate.queryForObject(sql, Long.class);
}
```

Saving a list of objects at once

In this recipe, we will add a DAO method to save a list of objects to the database efficiently.

How to do it...

Use the `batchUpdate()` method that takes an SQL `insert` query and a list of values as parameters:

```
public void add(List<User> userList) {
    String sql = "insert into user (first_name, age) values (?, ?)";

    List<Object[]> userRows = new ArrayList<Object[]>();
    for (User user : userList) {
        userRows.add(new Object[] {user.getFirstName(),
user.getAge()});
    }

    jdbcTemplate.batchUpdate(sql, userRows);
}
```

How it works...

A list of SQL `insert` queries will be generated from the SQL `insert` query string and the list of values. They will be sent to the database and committed all at once.

Reverting incomplete database modifications using transactions

Some database modifications involve several SQL queries, for example, inserting an object with attributes spread across several tables. If one of the queries fails, we would want to undo any previous ones that were successful.

How to do it...

Here are the steps to make DAO methods transactional:

1. Add `@EnableTransactionManagement` to the Spring configuration class:

```
@Configuration
@EnableWebMvc
@EnableTransactionManagement
@ComponentScan(basePackages =
{"com.spring_cookbook.controllers",
"com.spring_cookbook.dao"})
public class AppConfig {
   ...
```

2. Add a `DataSourceTransactionManager` bean to the Spring configuration:

```
@Bean
public DataSourceTransactionManager transactionManager() {
    DataSourceTransactionManager transactionManager = new
DataSourceTransactionManager();
   transactionManager.setDataSource(dataSource());
   return transactionManager;
}
```

3. Annotate the DAO class with `@Transactional`:

```
@Repository
@Transactional
public class UserDAO {
   ...
```

How it works...

`@Transactional` will enclose each DAO method in a `BEGIN...COMMIT` SQL block. So if there's an error (a runtime exception), any modification made by the DAO method to the database will be rolled back.

Using Hibernate for powerful object persistence and querying

In this recipe, you will learn how to use Hibernate with Spring. We'll use a MySQL database.

Getting ready

In this recipe, we'll use a MySQL database with the `user` table:

```
CREATE TABLE user (
  id int NOT NULL AUTO_INCREMENT,
  first_name text,
  age int DEFAULT NULL,
  PRIMARY KEY (id)
);
```

We'll use this corresponding JPA-annotated domain class:

```
@Entity
@Table(name = "user")
public class User {

  @Id
  @GeneratedValue
  private Long id;

  @Column(name = "first_name")
  private String firstName;

  private Integer age;

  // getters and setters..
```

For more information about the **Java Persistence API** (**JPA**), go to: `http://docs.oracle.com/javaee/6/tutorial/doc/bnbpz.html`.

How to do it...

Here are the steps to integrate Hibernate with Spring:

1. Add the Maven dependencies for Spring ORM, Hibernate, and the JDBC driver for MySQL in `pom.xml`:

    ```
    <dependency>
      <groupId>org.springframework</groupId>
      <artifactId>spring-orm</artifactId>
      <version>4.1.6.RELEASE</version>
    </dependency>

    <dependency>
    ```

```
    <groupId>mysql</groupId>
    <artifactId>mysql-connector-java</artifactId>
    <version>5.1.35</version>
</dependency>

<dependency>
    <groupId>org.hibernate</groupId>
    <artifactId>hibernate-core</artifactId>
    <version>4.3.8.Final</version>
</dependency>
```

2. Add `@EnableTransactionManagement` to the Spring configuration class:

```
@Configuration
@EnableWebMvc
@EnableTransactionManagement
@ComponentScan(basePackages =
{"com.spring_cookbook.controllers",
"com.spring_cookbook.dao"})
public class AppConfig {
...
```

3. In the Spring configuration, add a `dataSource` bean with the database connection details:

```
@Bean
public DataSource dataSource() {
        DriverManagerDataSource dataSource = new
DriverManagerDataSource();

        dataSource.setDriverClassName("com.mysql.jdbc.Driver");
        dataSource.setUrl("jdbc:mysql://localhost:3306/db1");
        dataSource.setUsername("user1");
        dataSource.setPassword("pass1");

        return dataSource;
}
```

4. In the Spring configuration class, add a `sessionFactory` bean method taking a `Datasource` object as an argument. In this bean method, we tell Hibernate to generate SQL code specific to MySQL and declare our `User` class:

```
@Bean
public SessionFactory sessionFactory(DataSource dataSource)
{
  LocalSessionFactoryBuilder sessionBuilder = new
LocalSessionFactoryBuilder(dataSource);
```

```
    Properties props = new Properties();
    props.put("hibernate.dialect",
"org.hibernate.dialect.MySQLDialect");
    props.put("hibernate.show_sql", "true");
    sessionBuilder.addProperties(props);

    sessionBuilder.addAnnotatedClass(User.class);

    return sessionBuilder.buildSessionFactory();
}
```

5. In the Spring configuration class, add a `HibernateTransactionManager` bean:

    ```
    @Bean
    public HibernateTransactionManager
    transactionManager(SessionFactory sessionFactory) {
      return new HibernateTransactionManager(sessionFactory);
    }
    ```

6. Add the `SessionFactory` bean to your DAO classes using dependency injection:

    ```
    @Autowired
    SessionFactory sessionFactory;
    ```

7. Use this `SessionFactory` bean to control Hibernate as usual, for example, this is a DAO method which will add a `User` object into the database:

    ```
    @Transactional
    public void add(User user) {
      sessionFactory.getCurrentSession().saveOrUpdate(user);
    }
    ```

5
Using Forms

In this chapter, we will cover the following recipes:

- ▶ Displaying and processing a form
- ▶ Getting a submitted form value using a controller method argument
- ▶ Setting a form's default values using a model object
- ▶ Saving form data in an object automatically
- ▶ Using text, textarea, password, and hidden fields
- ▶ Using a select field
- ▶ Using a checkbox
- ▶ Using a list of checkboxes
- ▶ Using a list of radio buttons
- ▶ Validating a form using annotations
- ▶ Uploading a file

Introduction

Displaying and processing a form is tedious. Spring helps with the initialization of the form, the generation of form widgets (text fields, checkboxes, and so on), and data retrieval when the form is submitted. Form validation is made simple with annotations in the model classes.

Displaying and processing a form

To display a form and retrieve the data the user entered when it's submitted, use a first controller method to display the form. Use a second controller method to process the form data when the form is submitted.

How to do it...

Here are the steps to display and process a form:

1. Create a controller method to display the form:

```
@RequestMapping("/addUser")
public String addUser() {
  return "addUser";
}
```

2. Create a JSP with an HTML form:

```
<form method="POST">
  <input type="text" name="firstName" />
  <input type="submit" />
</form>
```

3. Create another controller method to process the form when it's submitted:

```
@RequestMapping(value="/addUser", method=RequestMethod.POST)
public String addUserSubmit(HttpServletRequest request) {
  String firstName = request.getParameter("firstName");
  ...
  return "redirect:/home";
}
```

How it works...

The first controller method displays the JSP containing the HTML form. For more details, refer to the *Using a JSP view* recipe in *Chapter 3*, *Using Controllers and Views*.

The HTML form contains one text field. It's submitted via POST. The form's action attribute is absent, so the form will be submitted to the current page URL (/addUser).

The second controller method is called when the form is submitted. The value of the firstName form field is retrieved using HttpServletRequest. At the end, we will redirect to /home.

Both controller methods are mapped to the same `/addUser` URL. The first method is called for HTTP `GET` requests. The second method is called for HTTP `POST` requests (because of `method=RequestMethod.POST`).

There's more...

The two controller methods could have different URLs. For example, `/addUser` and `/addUserSubmit`. In this case, in the JSP, we would use the `action` attribute:

```
<form method="POST" action="/addUserSubmit">
   ...
</form>
```

See also

In the second controller method, to avoid using the cumbersome `request.getParameter()` method for each form field, refer to the *Getting a submitted form value using a controller method argument* and *Saving form values into an object automatically* recipes.

Getting a submitted form value using a controller method argument

In this recipe, you will learn how to get the submitted form data using controller method arguments. This is convenient for simple forms that are not related to a domain object.

How to do it...

Add an argument annotated with `@RequestParam` to the controller method:

```
@RequestMapping("processForm")
public void processForm(@RequestParam("name") String userName) {
    . . .
```

How it works...

The `userName` argument is initialized by Spring with the submitted value of the `name` form field.

`@RequestParam` can also retrieve URL parameters, for example, `http://localhost:8080/springwebapp/processForm?name=Merlin`.

There's more...

It's also possible to add the standard `HttpServletRequest` object as an argument of the controller method and get the submitted value for `name` directly from it:

```
@RequestMapping("processForm")
public void processForm(HttpServletRequest request) {
   String name = request.getParameter("name");
```

See also

Refer to the *Saving form values into an object automatically* recipe for more details.

Setting a form's default values using a model object

In this recipe, you will learn how to display a form with initial values that the user can change.

How to do it...

Create an object containing the default values in the controller. In the view, use Spring form tags to generate the form using that object:

1. In the controller, add a method annotated with `@ModelAttribute`, which returns an object with default values:

    ```
    @ModelAttribute("defaultUser")
    public User defaultUser() {
      User user = new User();
      user.setFirstName("Joe");
      user.setAge(18);
      return user;
    }
    ```

2. In the controller, add a method to display the form:

    ```
    @RequestMapping("addUser")
    public String addUser() {
      return "addUser";
    }
    ```

3. In the JSP, use Spring form tags to generate the form:

```
<%@ taglib prefix="form" uri="http://www.springframework.org/tags/form" %>

<form:form method="POST" modelAttribute="defaultUser">
  <form:input path="firstName" />
  <form:input path="age" />
  <input type="submit" value="Submit" />
</form:form>
```

How it works...

In the controller, because of `@ModelAttribute`, the `defaultUser()` method is automatically called for each request of the controller. The returned `User` object is stored in the memory as `defaultUser`. In the JSP, `defaultUser` is used to initialize the form:

▶ It's set as `modelAttribute` of the `form:form` element:

```
<form:form method="POST" modelAttribute="defaultUser">
```

▶ Form fields get their values from the corresponding properties of `defaultUser`. For example, the `firstName` field will be initialized with the value returned by `defaultUser.getFirstName()`.

Saving form data in an object automatically

For forms directly related to a model object, for example, a form to add `User`, the submitted form data can be automatically saved in an instance of that object.

How to do it...

In the controller method processing the form submission, add the object as an argument and make the field names in the JSP match its attributes:

1. Add a `User` argument annotated with `@ModelAttribute` to the controller method processing the form submission:

```
@RequestMapping(value="addUser", method=RequestMethod.POST)
public void addUser(@ModelAttribute User user) {
    ...
```

2. In the JSP, make sure that the form fields correspond to the existing attributes of the object:

```
<form:input path="firstName" />
<form:input path="age" />
```

How it works...

When the form is submitted, this is what goes on behind the scenes:

- ▶ A new `User` object is created
- ▶ The form values are injected into the object by matching the form field names to object attribute names, for example:

```
user.setFirstName(request.getParameter("firstName"));
```

- ▶ The resulting object is given to the controller method through its `@ModelAttribute` argument

There's more...

Instead of making Spring create a new object, you can provide the name of a default one:

```
public void addUser(@ModelAttribute("defaultUser") User user) {
...
```

In this case, Spring will use the object returned by the corresponding `@ModelAttribute` method of the controller class to store the submitted form data:

```
@ModelAttribute("defaultUser")
public User user() {
  User user = new User();
  user.setFirstName("Joe");
  user.setAge(18);
  return user;
}
```

Using text, textarea, password, and hidden fields

In this recipe, you will learn how to display a text field, `textarea` field, `password` field, and `hidden` field using Spring form tags. When the form is submitted, we will retrieve the field value in a controller method.

How to do it...

Here are the steps to display and process text fields:

1. If a default value is necessary, use a `String` attribute of the default object (refer to the *Setting a form's default values using a model object* recipe):

   ```
   user.setFirstName("Joe");
   ```

2. In the JSP, use one of these Spring form tags:

   ```
   <form:input path="firstName" />
   <form:textarea path="firstName" />
   <form:password path="firstName" />
   <form:hidden path="firstName" />
   ```

3. In the controller method processing the form submission, make sure that the @ `ModelAttribute` object has a corresponding `String` attribute:

   ```
   public class User {
     private String firstName;
   . . .
   ```

How it works...

The Spring form tag generates the HTML form field and populates it with the default value defined in the default object. The `path` attribute corresponds to the attribute of the default object. When the form is submitted, the form field value is saved in the corresponding attribute of the `@ModelAttribute` object.

For reference, this is the generated HTML code:

```
<input id="firstName" name="firstName" type="text" value="Joe"/>
<textarea id="firstName" name="firstName">Joe</textarea>
<input id="firstName" name="firstName" type="password" value=""/>
<input id="firstName" name="firstName" type="hidden" value="Joe"/>
```

 Note that the default value is not actually used for the `password` field.

Using a select field

In this recipe, you will learn how to display a `select` field. When the form is submitted, retrieve the selected value in a controller method.

How to do it...

1. In the controller, add a `@ModelAttribute` method returning a `Map` object that contains the `select` field options:

```
@ModelAttribute("countries")
public Map<String, String>countries() {
  Map<String, String> m = new HashMap<String, String>();
  m.put("us", "United States");
  m.put("ca", "Canada");
  m.put("fr", "France");
  m.put("de", "Germany");
  return m;
}
```

2. If a default value is necessary, use a `String` attribute of the default object (refer to the *Setting a form's default values using a model object* recipe) initialized with one of the `Map` keys:

```
user.setCountry("ca");
```

3. In the JSP, use a `form:select` element initialized with the `@ModelAttribute` Map:

```
<form:select path="country" items="${countries}" />
```

4. In the controller that processes the form submission, make sure that the `@ModelAttribute` object (the one used to save the form values) has a corresponding `String` attribute:

```
public class User {
  private String country;
  . . .
```

How it works...

The `form:select` tag generates an HTML `select` field and initializes it with the `@ModelAttribute` Map and the default value defined in the default object. The `path` attribute corresponds to the attribute of the default object. When the form is submitted, the selected value is saved in the corresponding attribute of the `@ModelAttribute User` object.

For reference, this is the generated HTML code:

```
<select id="country" name="country">
  <option value="de">Germany</option>
  <option value="fr">France</option>
  <option value="us">United States</option>
  <option value="ca" selected="selected">Canada</option>
</select>
```

There's more...

It's not necessary to use a `Map` class for the `@ModelAttribute` object. A `List<String>` object or directly using fields of an existing class may be more convenient.

Using a List<String> object

Instead of `Map`, it's possible that you can use a `List<String>` object:

```
@ModelAttribute("countries")
public List<String>countries() {
  List<String> l = new LinkedList<String>();
  l.add("com");
  l.add("ca");
  l.add("fr");
  l.add("de");
  return l;
}
```

The JSP code stays the same:

```
<form:select path="country" items="${countries}" />
```

In the generated HTML code, the displayed text will be the same as the `value` attribute:

```
<select id="country" name="country">
  <option value="com">com</option>
  <option value="ca" selected="selected">ca</option>
  <option value="fr">fr</option>
  <option value="de">de</option>
</select>
```

Using a List<Object> object

Instead of a `Map` object, you can use a `List<Object>` object. If, for example, `Country` was a class with `code` and `name` `String` attributes:

```
@ModelAttribute("countries")
public List<Country>countries() {
...
```

The JSP code would specify these attributes:

```
<form:select path="country" items="${countries}"
itemValue="code" itemLabel="name" />
```

The generated HTML code would be the same:

```
<select id="country" name="country">
  <option value="de">Germany</option>
  <option value="fr">France</option>
  <option value="us">United States</option>
  <option value="ca" selected="selected">Canada</option>
</select>
```

Using a checkbox

In this recipe, you will learn how to display a checkbox and, when the form is submitted, retrieve its state (selected or not) in a controller method.

How to do it...

Use the `form:checkbox` element in the JSP and a `boolean` attribute to store its value when the form is submitted:

1. If a default value is necessary, use a `boolean` attribute of the default object (refer to the *Setting a form's default values using a model object* recipe):

   ```
   user.setMarried(false);
   ```

2. In the JSP, use the `form:checkbox` element:

   ```
   <form:checkbox path="married" />
   ```

3. In the controller that processes the form submission, make sure that the @ `ModelAttribute` object has a corresponding `boolean` attribute:

   ```
   public class User {
     private boolean married;
   ...
   ```

How it works...

This is the generated HTML code:

```
<input id="married1" name="married" type="checkbox" value="true"/>
<input type="hidden" name="_married" value="on"/>
```

If the checkbox is checked, `married=true` is sent when the form is submitted. If it's not checked, nothing is sent (this is the standard HTML behavior). That's why a `hidden` form field is also generated. The field `_married` will be sent with the value `on` regardless of the checkbox state. So, if the married field is not there, Spring will know to set its value to false.

Using a list of checkboxes

In this recipe, you'll learn how to display a list of checkboxes and when the form is submitted, how to retrieve the selected values in a controller method.

How to do it...

1. In the controller, add a `@ModelAttribute` method returning a `Map` object:

```
@ModelAttribute("languages")
public Map<String, String>languages() {
  Map<String, String> m = new HashMap<String, String>();
  m.put("en", "English");
  m.put("fr", "French");
  m.put("de", "German");
  m.put("it", "Italian");
  return m;
}
```

2. If a default value is necessary, use a `String[]` attribute of the default object (refer to the *Setting a form's default values using a model object* recipe) initialized with some of the `Map` keys:

```
String[] defaultLanguages = {"en", "fr"};
user.setLanguages(defaultLanguages);
```

3. In the JSP, use a `form:checkboxes` element initialized with the `@ModelAttribute` Map:

```
<form:checkboxes items="${languages}" path="languages" />
```

In the controller that processes the form submission, make sure that the `@ModelAttribute` object (the one used to save the form values) has a corresponding `String[]` attribute:

```
public class User {
  private String[] languages;
...
```

How it works...

Spring's `form:checkboxes` tag generates the checkboxes using the `Map` keys as values and the `Map` values as text displayed to the user.

For reference, this is the generated HTML code:

```
<span>
  <input id="languages1" name="languages" type="checkbox" value="de"/>
  <label for="languages1">German</label>
</span>
<span>
  <input id="languages2" name="languages" type="checkbox" value="en"/>
  <label for="languages2">English</label>
</span>
<span>
  <input id="languages3" name="languages" type="checkbox" value="fr"/>
  <label for="languages3">French</label>
</span>

<input type="hidden" name="_languages" value="on"/>
```

As in the previous recipe, a `hidden` form field is also generated. `_languages=on` will be sent regardless of the checkboxes state. So, if none are selected, Spring will know to set the value of the languages array to an empty `String[]` object.

There's more...

To have more control on the generated HTML code (to avoid the `label` and `span` tags), it's possible to use several `form:checkbox` elements with the same value for the `path` attribute:

```
<form:checkbox path="languages" value="de" />German
<form:checkbox path="languages" value="en" />English
<form:checkbox path="languages" value="fr" />French
```

The generated HTML code is similar, except for the `hidden` attribute, which is generated multiple times:

```
<input id="languages1" name="languages" type="checkbox" value="de"/>
<input type="hidden" name="_languages" value="on"/>
German

<input id="languages2" name="languages" type="checkbox" value="en"/>
<input type="hidden" name="_languages" value="on"/>
English

<input id="languages3" name="languages" type="checkbox" value="fr"/>
<input type="hidden" name="_languages" value="on"/>
French
```

Using a list of radio buttons

In this recipe, you'll learn how to display a list of radio buttons. When the form is submitted, retrieve the selected value in a controller method.

How to do it...

1. In the controller, add a `@ModelAttribute` method returning `Map` object:

```
@ModelAttribute("countries")
public Map<String, String>countries() {
  Map<String, String> m = new HashMap<String, String>();
  m.put("us", "United States");
  m.put("ca", "Canada");
  m.put("fr", "France");
  m.put("de", "Germany");
  return m;
}
```

2. If a default value is necessary, use a `String` attribute of the default object (refer to the *Setting a form's default values using a model object* recipe) initialized with one of the `Map` keys:

```
user.setCountry("ca");
```

3. In the JSP, use a `form:radiobuttons` element initialized with the `@ModelAttribute` Map:

```
<form:radiobuttons items="${countries}" path="country" />
```

4. In the controller processing the form submission, make sure that the @ModelAttribute object (the one used to save the form values) has a corresponding String attribute:

```
public class User {
  private String country;
  . . .
```

How it works...

Spring's form:radiobuttons tag generates the radio buttons using the Map keys as values and the Map values as text displayed to the user.

For reference, this is the generated HTML code:

```
<span>
  <input id="country1" name="country" type="radio" value="de"/>
  <label for="country1">Germany</label>
</span>
<span>
  <input id="country2" name="country" type="radio" value="fr"/>
  <label for="country2">France</label>
</span>
<span>
  <input id="country3" name="country" type="radio" value="us"/>
  <label for="country3">United States</label>
</span>
<span>
  <input id="country4" name="country" type="radio" value="ca"
checked="checked"/>
  <label for="country4">Canada</label>
</span>
```

There's more...

To have more control of the generated HTML code (to avoid the label and span tags), it's possible to use several form:radiobutton elements with the same value for the path attribute:

```
<form:radiobutton path="country" value="de" />Germany
<form:radiobutton path="country" value="fr" />France
<form:radiobutton path="country" value="us" />United States
<form:radiobutton path="country" value="ca" />Canada
```

The generated HTML code for the input fields is identical to the code generated by the `form:radiobutton` tag:

```
<input id="country1" name="country" type="radio" value="de"/>Germany
<input id="country2" name="country" type="radio" value="fr"/>France
<input id="country3" name="country" type="radio" value="us"/>United
States
<input id="country4" name="country" type="radio" value="ca"
checked="checked"/>Canada
```

Validating a form using annotations

In this recipe, you'll learn how to add form validation rules by adding constraints directly in model classes using annotations. For example:

```
public class User {
   @NotEmpty
   private String firstName;
```

We'll use constraint annotations from the Java bean annotation API and from Hibernate Validator (which is a project independent of Hibernate ORM).

If the validation fails, the form will be shown again to the user with the errors that are to be fixed.

How to do it...

Add constraint annotations to the model class. Check whether the validation was successful in the controller method. Add error tags in the JSP:

1. Add the Maven dependencies in `pom.xml`:

```
<dependency>
  <groupId>javax.validation</groupId>
  <artifactId>validation-api</artifactId>
  <version>1.1.0.Final</version>
</dependency>

<dependency>
  <groupId>org.hibernate</groupId>
  <artifactId>hibernate-validator</artifactId>
  <version>5.1.2.Final</version>
</dependency>
```

2. Add constraints using annotations to the model class:

```
@NotEmpty
private String firstName;

@Min(18) @Max(130)
private int age;
```

3. In the controller method processing the form submission, add `@Valid` to the result object argument and a `BindingResult` argument after it:

```
@RequestMapping(value="addUser", method=RequestMethod.POST)
public void addUser(@ModelAttribute("defaultUser") @Valid
User user, BindingResult result) {
...
```

4. In that same controller method, check whether the validation was successful:

```
if(result.hasErrors()) {
  // show the form page again, with the errors
  return "addUser";
}
else {
  // validation was successful, redirect to another page
  return "redirect:/home";
}
```

5. Add form errors tags in the form JSP:

```
<form:input path="firstName" />
<form:errors path="firstName" cssclass="error"></form:errors>

<form:input path="age" />
<form:errors path="age" cssclass="error"></form:errors>
```

How it works...

The constraint annotations in the model class are used to validate the `User` object when the form is submitted. The errors are stored in the `BindingResult` object. When the form is displayed again, the `form:errors` elements will display them. An example of the generated HTML code with the errors is as follows:

```
<input id="firstName" name="firstName" type="text" value=""/>
<span id="firstName.errors" cssclass="error">may not be empty</span>

<input id="age" name="age" type="text" value="1233"/>
<span id="age.errors" cssclass="error">must be less than or equal to
120</span>
```

There's more...

Some common constraint annotations are:

- ▶ @Max(120): This field must have a value lower than or equal to the given number
- ▶ @Min(18): This field must have a value equal to or greater than the given number
- ▶ @NotNull: This field must not be null
- ▶ @Valid: This field must be a valid object
- ▶ @NotBlank: This String field must not be null and its trimmed length must be greater than 0
- ▶ @NotEmpty: This collection field must not be null nor empty

A full list of all the constraint annotations can be found here:

- ▶ http://docs.oracle.com/javaee/6/tutorial/doc/gircz.html
- ▶ http://docs.jboss.org/hibernate/stable/validator/reference/en-US/html_single/#section-builtin-constraints

To create a custom constraint annotation, refer to:

http://docs.jboss.org/hibernate/stable/validator/reference/en-US/html_single/#validator-customconstraints.

Uploading a file

To allow a user to upload a file from an HTML form, we need to set the form encoding to multipart/form-data. On the server side, we will use the fileupload package from the Apache Commons library to process the uploaded file.

How to do it...

Here are the steps to upload a file from a form:

1. Add the Maven dependency for fileupload from Apache Commons in pom.xml:

```
<dependency>
  <groupId>commons-fileupload</groupId>
  <artifactId>commons-fileupload</artifactId>
  <version>1.3.1</version>
</dependency>
```

2. In the Spring configuration, declare a `MultipartResolver` bean with a size limit (in bytes) for the data to be uploaded:

```
@Bean
MultipartResolver multipartResolver() {
  CommonsMultipartResolver resolver = new
CommonsMultipartResolver();
  resolver.setMaxUploadSize(500000000);
  return resolver;
}
```

3. In the JSP, set the HTML form encoding to `multipart/form-data`:

```
<form:form method="POST" modelAttribute="defaultUser"
enctype="multipart/form-data">
```

4. Add a file upload widget:

```
<input type="file" name="file" />
```

5. In the controller method processing the form submission, add `MultipartFile` as a `@RequestParam` argument:

```
@RequestMapping(value="addUser", method=RequestMethod.POST)
public void addUser(User user, @RequestParam("file")
MultipartFile formFile) {
    ...
```

6. Save the uploaded file to a `files` folder in the `Tomcat` directory:

```
try {
    // Create the folder "files" if necessary
    String tomcatFolderPath =
System.getProperty("catalina.home");
    File filesFolder = new File(tomcatFolderPath +
File.separator + "files");
    if ( ! filesFolder.exists()) {
        filesFolder.mkdirs();
    }

    // Write the uploaded file
    File file = new File(filesFolder.getAbsolutePath() +
File.separator + formFile.getName());
    BufferedOutputStream fileStream = new
BufferedOutputStream(new FileOutputStream(file));
    fileStream.write(formFile.getBytes());
    fileStream.close();
```

```
} catch (Exception e) {
  // deal with the exception…
}
```

How it works...

In the JSP, the `multipart/form-data` encoding is necessary for the form to be able to encode and send files.

In the controller, we will create the `files` folder if it doesn't exist. At this point, the uploaded file is in the server's memory. We still need to write it to the filesystem. We do that using the `formFile` argument. Note that if a file with the same name already exists, it will be overwritten.

There's more...

To upload several files, you can have several form fields (file1, file2 and so on) and their corresponding arguments (formFile1, formFile2 and so on). It's also possible to use the same field name for multiple file upload widgets (this is convenient to allow the user to upload an undetermined number of files):

```
<input type="file" name="file" />
<input type="file" name="file" />
<input type="file" name="file" />
```

In this case, we'll retrieve the files as an array of `MultipartFile` in the controller method:

```
@RequestMapping(value="addUser", method=RequestMethod.POST)
public void addUser(User user, @RequestParam("file")
MultipartFile[] formFileArray) {
    ...
```

6

Managing Security

In this chapter, we will cover the following recipes:

- ▶ Enabling Spring Security
- ▶ Authenticating users using the default login page
- ▶ Authenticating users using a custom login page
- ▶ Authenticating users using a database
- ▶ Adding a logout link
- ▶ Using public folders
- ▶ Authorizing only users with a specific role to view some pages
- ▶ Displaying page elements only to authenticated users in views
- ▶ Using HTTPS with Tomcat

Introduction

In this chapter, we'll cover the basics of managing the security of a Spring web application using **user authentication**, **user authorization**, and **HTTPS**.

User authentication is all about identifying a user: usually through a username and a password. User authorization is about assigning roles to users. These roles are then used at runtime to determine whether a user is allowed to perform a given action or view some specific contents. User authentication and authorization are handled by Spring.

HTTPS is all about encrypting the communication between our web server and the user's browser using **Secure Sockets Layer** (**SSL**). HTTPS needs to be enabled at the server level. We'll see how to do this with Tomcat.

The first recipe, *Enabling Spring Security*, is required for any of the other recipes to work.

Enabling Spring Security

To enable Spring Security, you need to add some Maven dependencies. You also need to create some configuration classes.

How to do it...

Here are the steps to enable Spring Security:

1. Add the Maven dependencies for Spring Security in `pom.xml`. Note that the version number is different from Spring Core:

```
<dependency>
    <groupId>org.springframework.security</groupId>
    <artifactId>spring-security-web</artifactId>
    <version>3.2.5.RELEASE</version>
</dependency>

<dependency>
    <groupId>org.springframework.security</groupId>
    <artifactId>spring-security-config</artifactId>
    <version>3.2.5.RELEASE</version>
</dependency>
```

2. Create a class for the Spring Security configuration:

```
@Configuration
@EnableWebSecurity
public class SecurityConfig extends
WebSecurityConfigurerAdapter {
}
```

3. Declare the configuration class in the `ServletInitializer` class:

```
public class ServletInitializer extends
AbstractAnnotationConfigDispatcherServletInitializer {

    @Override
    protected Class<?>[] getRootConfigClasses() {
```

```
        return new Class[] {SecurityConfig.class};
    }

    . . .
```

4. Add a class implementing `AbstractSecurityWebApplicationInitializer` to initialize Spring Security's servlet filter:

```
public class SecurityWebApplicationInitializer extends
AbstractSecurityWebApplicationInitializer {

}
```

How it works...

`SecurityWebApplicationInitializer` registers, behind the scenes, a servlet filter, which will handle access to any URL of the web application.

The `SecurityConfig` class will be loaded at startup (because of its declaration in `ServletInitializer`). The Spring configuration code that we will write in the following recipes will go in the `SecurityConfig` class.

Authenticating users using the default login page

Spring makes it easy to quickly add a login page to your web application; just define some user credentials (usernames and passwords) in the security configuration class. To access any page, the user will have to go through Spring's default login page first.

How to do it...

In your security configuration class, add a `configureUsers()` method containing the hardcoded user credentials:

```
@Configuration
@EnableWebSecurity
public class SecurityConfig extends WebSecurityConfigurerAdapter {
    @Autowired
    public void configureUsers(AuthenticationManagerBuilder auth)
throws Exception {
        auth.inMemoryAuthentication()
.withUser("user1").password("pwd").roles("USER")
    .and()
.withUser("admin").password("admin_pwd").roles("USER", "ADMIN");

    }
}
```

How it works...

In `configureUsers()`, we told Spring to use the provided user credentials for user authentication. We assigned roles to each user. A role is an arbitrary `String` object. To use those roles for authorization, refer to the *Authorizing only users with a specific role to view some pages,* recipe.

By default, the Spring's default login page will be used to protect all the pages of the web application. This is defined in the default `configure()` method of Spring Security:

```
protected void configure(HttpSecurity http) throws Exception {
  http
      .authorizeRequests()
          .anyRequest().authenticated()
      .and().formLogin()
      .and().httpBasic();
}
```

We will override this method in the following recipe in order to define a custom login page.

Authenticating users using a custom login page

In this recipe, you'll learn how to build your own login form instead of using Spring's default login form.

How to do it...

Here are the steps to define a custom login page:

1. Make sure that the JSTL Maven dependency is declared in `pom.xml`:

```
<dependency>
    <groupId>javax.servlet</groupId>
    <artifactId>jstl</artifactId>
    <version>1.2</version>
</dependency>
```

2. Make sure that a JSP view resolver is declared in the `AppConfig` class:

```
@Bean
public ViewResolver jspViewResolver(){
    InternalResourceViewResolver resolver = new
InternalResourceViewResolver();
    resolver.setViewClass(JstlView.class);
    resolver.setPrefix("/WEB-INF/jsp/");
    resolver.setSuffix(".jsp");
    return resolver;
}
```

3. Add a controller method for the login page in a controller class:

```
@Controller
public class UserController {

  @RequestMapping("login")
  public String login() {
      return "login";
  }
  ...
```

4. Add a JSP for the login page:

```
<%@ page language="java" contentType="text/html;
charset=UTF-8" pageEncoding="UTF-8"%>
<%@ taglib prefix="c"
uri="http://java.sun.com/jsp/jstl/core" %>
<%@ taglib prefix="form"
uri="http://www.springframework.org/tags/form" %>
<%@ page isELIgnored="false" %>

<c:url var="loginUrl" value="/login" />
<form action="${loginUrl}" method="post">
    <input type="hidden" name="${_csrf.parameterName}"
value="${_csrf.token}"/>

    <c:if test="${param.error != null}">
        <p>
            Invalid username and password.
        </p>
    </c:if>

    <p>
        <label for="username">Username</label>
        <input type="text" id="username" name="username"/>
    </p>

    <p>
        <label for="password">Password</label>
        <input type="password" id="password"
name="password"/>
    </p>


    <button type="submit">Log in</button>
</form>
```

5. In the `SecurityConfig` class, override the Spring's default `configure()` method. Declare the URL of your custom login page:

```
protected void configure(HttpSecurity http) throws Exception {
    http.authorizeRequests().anyRequest().authenticated();
    http.formLogin().loginPage("/login").permitAll();
}
```

How it works...

In the `SecurityConfig` class, the `configure()` method:

► Requires authentication for any URL: `anyRequest().authenticated()`

► Allows user authentication through the custom login page: `formLogin().loginPage("/login")`

► Allows anyone access to the login page: `loginPage("/login").permitAll();`

Authenticating users using a database

In this recipe, you'll learn how to use user credentials (username and password) from a database for authentication.

How to do it...

Here are the steps to use user credentials in a database for authentication:

1. Add the Spring JDBC Maven dependency in `pom.xml`:

```
<dependency>
    <groupId>org.springframework</groupId>
    <artifactId>spring-jdbc</artifactId>
    <version>${spring.version}</version>
</dependency>
```

2. In the database, create the `users` and `authorities` tables:

```
create table users(
  username varchar(50) not null,
  password varchar(50) not null,
  enabled boolean not null default true,
  primary key (username)
);

create table authorities (
```

```
    username varchar(50) not null,
    authority varchar(50) not null,
    constraint fk_authorities_users foreign key(username)
references users(username)
);

create unique index ix_auth_username on authorities
(username,authority);
```

3. In the database, add users and their roles:

```
insert into users (username, password) values
('user1','pwd1');
insert into users (username, password) values
('user2','pwd2');

insert into authorities (username, authority) values
('user1', 'ADMIN');
insert into authorities (username, authority) values
('user2', 'ADMIN');
```

4. In the `SecurityConfig` class, add a `DataSource` bean with the database connection details:

```
@Bean
public DataSource dataSource() {
        DriverManagerDataSource dataSource = new
DriverManagerDataSource();

dataSource.setDriverClassName("com.mysql.jdbc.Driver");
dataSource.setUrl("jdbc:mysql://localhost:3306/db1");
        dataSource.setUsername("user1");
        dataSource.setPassword("pass1");

        return dataSource;
}
```

5. In the `SecurityConfig` class, add a `DataSourceTransactionManager` bean:

```
@Bean
public DataSourceTransactionManager transactionManager() {
    DataSourceTransactionManager transactionManager = new
DataSourceTransactionManager();
    transactionManager.setDataSource(dataSource());
    return transactionManager;
}
```

6. In the `SecurityConfig` class, override the Spring's `configure()` method:

```
@Autowired
public void configure(AuthenticationManagerBuilder auth)
throws Exception {
    auth.jdbcAuthentication()
            .dataSource(dataSource())
            .usersByUsernameQuery(
                    "select username,password,enabled from
users where username=?")
            .authoritiesByUsernameQuery(
                    "select username,authority from
authorities where username=?");
}
```

How it works...

With the `configure()` method overridden, Spring Security will:

▶   Use JDBC for authentication

▶   Use the provided `DataSource` bean to connect to the database

▶   Perform these SQL queries to get users and their roles

Adding a logout link

In this recipe, you'll learn how to add a URL `/logout` to let the user log out.

How to do it...

In the `SecurityConfig` class, in the `configure()` method, call the `logout()` method and the `logoutRequestMatcher()` method to declare a logout URL:

```
protected void configure(HttpSecurity http) throws Exception {
    ...
    AntPathRequestMatcher pathRequestMatcher = new
AntPathRequestMatcher("/logout");
    http.logout().logoutRequestMatcher(pathRequestMatcher);
}
```

Use `org.springframework.security.web.util.` **`matcher`**`.AntPathRequestMatcher`, and not the deprecated `org.springframework.security.web.util.` `AntPathRequestMatcher` class.

How it works...

While going to the URL `/logout`, the user will be logged out.

Using public folders

Some folders need their contents to be accessible without authentication, for example, the folder containing CSS files, the folder containing JavaScript files, and the folder containing static images. None of these usually contain confidential information and some of their files may be necessary to display the login page and the public pages of the website properly.

How to do it...

In the security configuration class, override the `configure(WebSecurity web)` method to define the public folders:

```
@Override
public void configure(WebSecurity web) throws Exception {
    web
        .ignoring()
          .antMatchers("/css/**")
          .antMatchers("/js/**");
          .antMatchers("/img/**");
}
```

There's more...

It's also possible to define them in the standard `configure()` method:

```
protected void configure(HttpSecurity http) throws Exception {
  http.authorizeRequests()
        .antMatchers("/css/**", "/js/**", "/img/**").permitAll()
        .anyRequest().authenticated();
}
```

This enables public access to these folders, but requires authentication for any other request.

Authorizing only users with a specific role to view some pages

There are pages that only a few users should be allowed to access. For example, admin pages should be accessible only to admin users. This is done by matching the URLs of these pages to user roles, which were defined when the users were created; refer to the *Authenticating users using the default login page* and *Authenticating users using a database* recipes.

How to do it...

In the `configure()` method, use the `hasRole()` method:

```
http.authorizeRequests()
    .antMatchers("/admin/**").hasRole("ADMIN")
    .anyRequest().authenticated();
```

How it works...

This allows access to URLs starting with the `/admin` path only to users with the `ADMIN` role.

Displaying page elements only to authenticated users in views

In this recipe, you'll learn how to display some elements of a page only to authenticated users. For example, a summary box with the information about the account of the currently logged-in user.

How to do it...

Use the `<sec:authorize>` tag in the JSP file to add conditions for some content to be displayed:

1. Add the Maven dependency for the Spring Security JSP tags library in `pom.xml`:

    ```
    <dependency>
      <groupId>org.springframework.security</groupId>
      <artifactId>spring-security-taglibs</artifactId>
      <version>3.2.5.RELEASE</version>
    </dependency>
    ```

2. In the JSP, declare the tag library and use `<sec:authorize>`:

```
<%@ taglib prefix="sec"
uri="http://www.springframework.org/security/tags" %>

<sec:authorize access="isAuthenticated()">
  Username: <sec:authentication
property="principal.username" />
</sec:authorize>
```

How it works...

The text in the `sec:authorize` tag will be displayed only for authenticated users. We used the `sec:authentication` tag to display the username of the currently logged-in user.

There's more...

To display contents only to the not-authenticated users, use the `isAnonymous()` function:

```
<sec:authorize access="isAnonymous()">
  This will be shown only to not-authenticated users.
</sec:authorize>
```

To display contents only to the users with the ADMIN role, use the `hasRole()` function.

```
<sec:authorize access="hasRole('ADMIN')">
  This will be shown only to users who have the "ADMIN" authority.
</sec:authorize>
```

To display contents to the users with the ADMIN role or the WARRIOR role, use the hasAnyRole() function.

```
<sec:authorize access="hasAnyRole('ADMIN', 'WARRIOR')">
  This will be shown only to users who have the "ADMIN" or the
"WARRIOR" authority.
</sec:authorize>
```

A full list of all the Spring expressions is available at:

http://docs.spring.io/spring-security/site/docs/3.0.x/reference/el-access.html.

Using HTTPS with Tomcat

To use HTTPS URLs, no Spring configuration is required, but you need to enable HTTPS on your server. In this recipe, we'll cover how to do this for Tomcat (on a Mac OS or Linux) using a self-generated SSL certificate. For production, remember to use a real commercial SSL certificate.

How to do it...

Here are the steps to enable HTTPS for Tomcat:

1. To generate an SSL certificate, open a Terminal and use the `keytool` command to create `certificate.bin`. In this example, the certificate user name is `admin` and the password is `adminpass`:

    ```
    keytool -genkey -alias admin -keypass adminpass -keystore
    certificate.bin -storepass adminpass
    ```

2. Accept the default values, except for the last question whose answer should be `yes`:

    ```
    What is your first and last name?
      [Unknown]:
    What is the name of your organizational unit?
      [Unknown]:
    What is the name of your organization?
      [Unknown]:
    What is the name of your City or Locality?
      [Unknown]:
    What is the name of your State or Province?
      [Unknown]:
    What is the two-letter country code for this unit?
      [Unknown]:
    Is CN=Unknown, OU=Unknown, O=Unknown, L=Unknown,
    ST=Unknown, C=Unknown correct?
      [no]:  yes
    ```

3. Move `certificate.bin` to the root of Tomcat's folder.

4. In `<tomcat_folder>/conf/server.xml`, uncomment the definition starting with `<Connector port="8443"` and add the `keystoreFile` and `keystorePass` attributes:

```
<Connector port="8443" protocol="HTTP/1.1" SSLEnabled="true"
           maxThreads="150" scheme="https" secure="true"
           clientAuth="false" sslProtocol="TLS"
           keystoreFile="certificate.bin"
keystorePass="adminpass" />
```

5. Restart Tomcat and make sure that your web application is available via HTTPS on the `8443` port: `https://localhost:8443`.

How it works...

We configured Tomcat to accept incoming HTTPS requests on the `8443` port using a self-signed SSL certificate. Most web browsers will display a security warning before displaying the page because the SSL certificate is self-signed.

There's more...

The `certificate.bin` file can be anywhere on the machine, just use an absolute path in `server.xml`.

It's possible to change the port number `8443` to anything else.

It's possible to use HTTPS exclusively by disabling access via plain HTTP; comment out the non-SSL connector in `server.xml`.

For more information about Tomcat and HTTPS/SSL, go to `https://tomcat.apache.org/tomcat-8.0-doc/ssl-howto.html`.

7

Unit Testing

In this chapter, we will cover the following recipes:

- ▸ Unit testing with JUnit 4
- ▸ Unit testing with TestNG 6
- ▸ Simulating dependencies with mocks using Mockito
- ▸ Unit testing with JUnit 4 using Spring's application context
- ▸ Unit testing with TestNG 6 using Spring's application context
- ▸ Unit testing with transactions
- ▸ Unit testing controller methods

Introduction

We often skip unit testing because we don't know how to do it or we believe that testing web applications is difficult. In fact, unit testing is easy and Spring makes web application testing effortless.

In this chapter, you will first learn how to write unit tests using JUnit, TestNG, and Mockito. Then, we will use Spring context, dependency injection, and transactions in our tests. Finally, we will test Spring controller methods using only a few lines of code.

Unit testing with JUnit 4

JUnit, first released in 2000, is the most widely used Java unit testing framework. Eclipse supports it out of the box.

In this recipe, we will write and execute a JUnit 4 test.

Getting ready

In this recipe, we'll test this simple method (located in the `NumberUtil` class), which adds two integers:

```
public static int add(int a, int b) {
  return a + b;
}
```

How to do it...

Follow these steps to test a method with JUnit 4:

1. Add the `junit` Maven dependency in `pom.xml`:

```
<dependency>
  <groupId>junit</groupId>
  <artifactId>junit</artifactId>
  <version>4.10</version>
  <scope>test</scope>
</dependency>
```

2. Create a Java package for your test classes. The standard practice is to keep the test classes in a separate folder with the same package structure. For example, the class we test, `NumberUtil`, is in the `src/main/java` folder, in the `com.spring_cookbook.util` package. Our corresponding test class will be in the `src/test/java` folder, which is also in a `com.spring_cookbook.util` package.

3. Create the test class; in Eclipse, in the **File** menu, select **New | JUnit Test Case**. We will use `NumberUtilTest` as class name.

4. Create the unit test method by replacing the default `test()` method with:

```
@Test
public void testAdd() {
  assertEquals(NumberUtil.add(5, 3), 8);
  assertEquals(NumberUtil.add(1500, 32), 1532);
}
```

5. Run the test in Eclipse; right-click somewhere in the class and choose **Run As | JUnit Test**.

6. You can also run the test with Maven if you used the folder and package structure described in step 2:

```
mvn test
```

How it works...

A JUnit class is a normal Java class with some methods annotated with `@Test`.

`assertEquals(x, y)` is a JUnit method that makes a test method fail if `x` is not equal to `y`.

In the `testAdd()` method, we check whether the method works for different sets of data.

There's more...

Some other useful JUnit method annotations are:

▸ `@Test(expected=Exception.class)`: This method is expected to throw this exception. For example, to make sure that some code throws this exception in a given situation.

▸ `@Before`: This method is executed before each test method of the test class is executed. For example, to reinitialize some class attributes used by the methods.

▸ `@After`: This method is executed after each test method of the test class is executed. For example, to roll back database modifications.

▸ `@BeforeClass`: This method is executed once before all test methods of the class are executed. For example, this method could contain some initialization code.

▸ `@AfterClass`: This method is executed once after all test methods of the class are executed. For example, this method could contain some cleanup code.

▸ `@Test(timeout=1000)`: The test fails if this method takes longer than 1 second. For example, to make sure that the execution time of some code stays under a certain duration.

Having a naming convention for test methods helps the code to be more maintainable and readable. To get some ideas about different naming conventions, you can visit

```
http://java.dzone.com/articles/7-popular-unit-test-naming.
```

Unit testing with TestNG 6

TestNG, first released in 2004, is the second most popular Java unit testing framework. With most of JUnit features, it also offers parameterized testing (executing a test method with different sets of data) and convenient features for integration testing.

In this recipe, we will write a parameterized test to test the same method as in the previous recipe.

Getting ready

In this recipe, we'll test this simple method (located in the `NumberUtil` class), which adds two integers:

```
public static int add(int a, int b) {
  return a + b;
}
```

How to do it...

Follow these steps to test a method with TestNG 6:

1. Add the `testng` Maven dependency in `pom.xml`:

   ```
   <dependency>
     <groupId>org.testng</groupId>
     <artifactId>testng</artifactId>
     <version>6.1.1</version>
     <scope>test</scope>
   </dependency>
   ```

2. In Eclipse, install the TestNG plugin. In the **Help** menu, select **Install New Software....** In the **Work with:** field, enter `http://beust.com/eclipse` and press the *Enter* key. Select **TestNG** below the **Work with:** field.

3. Create a Java package for your test classes. The standard practice is to have test classes in a separate folder with the same package structure. For example, the class we test, `NumberUtil`, is in the `src/main/java` folder, in the `com.spring_cookbook.util` package. Our corresponding test class will be in the `src/test/java` folder, also in a `com.spring_cookbook.util` package.

4. Create the `NumberUtilTest` TestNG test class:

```
import static org.testng.Assert.*;

public class NumberUtilTest {


}
```

5. Add a `@DataProvider` method with multiple datasets:

```
@DataProvider
public Object[][] values() {
return new Object[][] {
   new Object[] { 1, 2, 3 },
   new Object[] { 4, 5, 9 },
   new Object[] { 3000, 2000, 5000 },
   new Object[] { 25, 50, 75 },
  };
```

6. Add the unit test method, which takes three integers and checks whether the addition of the first two gives the third:

```
@Test(dataProvider = "values")
public void testAdd(int a, int b, int c) {
   assertEquals(NumberUtil.add(a, b), c);
}
```

7. Run the test in Eclipse; right-click somewhere in the class and choose **Run As | TestNG Test**.

8. You can also run the test with Maven if you used the folder and package structure described in step3:

```
mvn test
```

How it works...

The `dataProvider` attribute of the `@Test` method will be used to test the method with the arrays from the `@DataProvider` method.

In the console, verify that the test method has been executed for each dataset:

```
PASSED: testAdd(1, 2, 3)
PASSED: testAdd(4, 5, 9)
PASSED: testAdd(3000, 2000, 5000)
```

There's more...

Some other useful TestNG method annotations are:

- ▶ `@Test(expectedExceptions=Exception.class)`: This method is expected to throw this exception. For example, to make sure some code throws this exception in a given situation.

- ▶ `@BeforeMethod`: This method is executed before each test method of the test class is executed. For example, to reinitialize some class attributes used by the methods.

- ▶ `@AfterMethod`: This method is executed after each test method of the test class is executed. For example, to roll back database modifications.

- ▶ `@BeforeClass`: This method is executed once before the test methods of the class are executed. For example, this method could contain some initialization code.

- ▶ `@AfterClass`: This method is executed once after all test methods of the class are executed. For example, this method could contain some cleanup code.

- ▶ `@Test(invocationTimeOut=1000)`: The test fails if this method takes longer than 1 second. For example, to make sure that the execution time of some code stays under a certain duration.

It's possible to execute a test only if another test was successful (useful for integration testing):

```java
@Test
public void connectToDatabase() {}

@Test(dependsOnMethods = { "connectToDatabase" })
public void testMyFancySQLQuery() {
    ...
}
```

Other advanced features are well explained in TestNG's documentation at `http://testng.org/doc/documentation-main.html#parameters-dataproviders`.

For more reasons to choose TestNG over JUnit, refer to `http://kaczanowscy.pl/tomek/sites/default/files/testng_vs_junit.txt.slidy_.html`.

Having a naming convention for test methods helps the code to be more maintainable and readable. You can find some ideas about different naming conventions at:

`http://java.dzone.com/articles/7-popular-unit-test-naming`.

Simulating dependencies with mocks using Mockito

With unit testing, as opposed to integration testing, we aim to test each class independently. However, many classes have dependencies that we don't want to rely on. So we use mocks.

Mocks are smart objects whose output can vary depending on the input. **Mockito** is the most popular mocking framework with a concise, yet easy to grasp, syntax.

Getting ready

We'll mock the `StringUtil` class with its `concat()` method concatenating two `String` objects:

```
public class StringUtil {
  public String concat(String a, String b) {
    return a + b;
  }
}
```

 Note that there's no good reason to mock this class, as it's just a convenient example, to show you how to use Mockito.

How to do it...

Follow these steps for simulating dependencies with mocks using Mockito:

1. Add the `mockito-core` Maven dependency in `pom.xml`:

```
<dependency>
  <groupId>org.mockito</groupId>
  <artifactId>mockito-core</artifactId>
  <version>1.10.8</version>
    <scope>test</scope>
</dependency>
```

2. In a test method, use Mockito to create a `mock` instance of `StringUtil`:

```
StringUtil stringUtilMock = Mockito.mock(StringUtil.class);
```

3. Program the mock:

```
Mockito.when(stringUtilMock.concat("a",
"b")).thenReturn("ab");
Mockito.when(stringUtilMock.concat("aa",
"bb")).thenReturn("aabb");
```

4. That's it. Let's check how the mock actually works now:

```
assertEquals(stringUtilMock.concat("a", "b"), "ab");
assertEquals(stringUtilMock.concat("aa", "bb"), "aabb");
```

How it works...

With the mock, we don't need the actual `StringUtil` class to execute our test method. Mockito creates and uses, behind the scenes, a proxy class.

Again, in the real world, creating a mock for this class would be overkill. Mocks are useful to simulate complicated dependencies, such as an SMTP method, the SMTP server behind it, or a REST service.

There's more...

It's easy to test whether the method was called exactly twice with `String` parameters:

```
Mockito.verify(stringUtilMock,
VerificationModeFactory.times(2)).concat(Mockito.anyString(),
Mockito.anyString());
```

Mockito offers many other similar methods:

```
VerificationModeFactory.atLeastOnce()
VerificationModeFactory.atLeast(minNumberOfInvocations)
VerificationModeFactory.atMost(maxNumberOfInvocations)

Mockito.anyObject()
Mockito.any(class)
Mockito.anyListOf(class)
```

It's also possible, at a given point, to reset the mock object's programmed behavior:

```
Mockito.reset(stringUtilMock);
```

For a more extensive list of Mockito's features, refer to `http://mockito.github.io/ mockito/docs/current/org/mockito/Mockito.html`.

Unit testing with JUnit 4 using Spring's application context

JUnit tests are run outside Spring; Spring is not initialized before the tests are run. To be able to use the beans defined in the configuration files and dependency injection, some bootstrapping code needs to be added to the test class.

How to do it...

Follow these steps to test a method using the Spring's application context with JUnit 4:

1. Add the `spring-test` Maven dependency in `pom.xml`:

    ```
    <dependency>
      <groupId>org.springframework</groupId>
      <artifactId>spring-test</artifactId>
      <version>4.1.1.RELEASE</version>
      <scope>test</scope>
    </dependency>
    ```

2. Add these annotations to the test class:

    ```
    @RunWith(SpringJUnit4ClassRunner.class)
    @ContextConfiguration(classes = {AppConfig.class})
    @WebAppConfiguration
    public class TestControllerTest {
        ...
    ```

3. Use Spring beans as usual, for example, as `@Autowired` fields:

    ```
    @Autowired
    private UserDAO userDAO;

    @Test
    public void testListUsers() {
      List<User> users = userDAO.findAll();
      ...
    }
    ```

How it works...

`@RunWith(SpringJUnit4ClassRunner.class)` executes the test with the Spring runner instead of the default JUnit runner. A runner is a class that runs a JUnit test.

`@ContextConfiguration(classes = {AppConfig.class})` loads the Spring configuration class and makes the class's beans available.

`@WebAppConfiguration` prevents exceptions from being raised. Without it, `@EnableWebMvc` (in the Spring configuration) would raise the "**A ServletContext is required to configure default servlet handling**" exception.

There's more...

You can choose to use a separate Spring configuration class to run your tests:

```
@ContextConfiguration(classes = {AppTestConfig.class})
```

You can also use the Spring main configuration class in combination with a test-specific configuration class:

```
@ContextConfiguration(classes = {AppConfig.class,
AppTestConfig.class})
```

The order in which the classes are declared matters. In this example, beans from `AppConfig` can be overridden in `AppTestConfig`. For example, you could choose to override a MySQL datasource by an in-memory database datasource for your tests.

Unit testing with TestNG 6 using Spring's application context

TestNG tests are run outside Spring; Spring is not initialized before the tests are run. To be able to use the beans defined in the configuration files and dependency injection, some bootstrapping code needs to be added to the test class.

How to do it...

Follow these steps to test a method using the Spring application context with TestNG 6:

1. Add the `spring-test` Maven dependency in `pom.xml`:

```
<dependency>
  <groupId>org.springframework</groupId>
  <artifactId>spring-test</artifactId>
  <version>4.1.1.RELEASE</version>
  <scope>test</scope>
</dependency>
```

2. Make the test class extend `AbstractTestNGSpringContextTests` and add these annotations to it:

```
@ContextConfiguration(classes = {AppConfig.class})
@WebAppConfiguration
public class TestControllerTest extends
AbstractTestNGSpringContextTests {
...
```

3. Use Spring beans as usual, for example, as `@Autowired` fields:

```
@Autowired
private UserDAO userDAO;

@Test
public void testListUsers() {
  List<User> users = userDAO.findAll();
  ...
}
```

How it works...

Extending `AbstractTestNGSpringContextTests` initializes Spring's context and makes it available to the test class.

`@ContextConfiguration(classes = {AppConfig.class})` loads the Spring configuration file in Spring's context.

`@WebAppConfiguration` prevents exceptions from being raised. Without it, `@EnableWebMvc` (in the Spring configuration) would raise the "**A ServletContext is required to configure default servlet handling**" exception.

There's more...

You can choose to use a separate Spring configuration class to run your tests:

```
@ContextConfiguration(classes = {AppTestConfig.class})
```

You can also use Spring's main configuration in combination with a test-specific configuration:

```
@ContextConfiguration(classes = {AppConfig.class,
AppTestConfig.class})
```

The order in which the classes are declared matters. In this example, beans from `AppConfig` can be overridden in `AppTestConfig`. For example, you could choose to override a MySQL datasource by an in-memory database datasource for your tests.

Unit testing with transactions

To test a DAO class, for example, you will need to perform database queries that won't be persisted. For example, to test the DAO method to add a user, you want to make sure that the user is actually created in the database, but you don't want that test user to remain in the database. Transactions help you to do this with minimum effort.

How to do it...

Follow these steps to automatically revert the database modifications performed by a test method:

With TestNG, make the test class extend:

```
public class UserDAOTest extends
AbstractTransactionalTestNGSpringContextTests {
...
```

With JUnit, add the @Transactional annotation to the test class:

```
@Transactional
public class UserDAOTest {
...
```

How it works...

Each test method of the class will automatically:

- ▶ Start a new transaction
- ▶ Execute as normal
- ▶ Rollback the transaction (so any modifications to a database will be reverted)

Unit testing controller methods

Unit testing the logic of controller methods is usually difficult, but Spring makes it easy by providing methods to simulate a request and test the response generated by Spring.

Getting ready

We'll test this controller method which concatenates two parameters and passes the result to the concat.jsp JSP file:

```
@RequestMapping("concat")
public String concat(@RequestParam String a, @RequestParam String
b, Model model) {
  String result = a + b;
  model.addAttribute("result", result);
  return "concat";
}
```

How to do it...

To test a controller method, build and execute an HTTP request and then perform tests on the response returned by the controller method. We will test that for a given set of parameters, the correct attribute is passed to the JSP and the user is redirected to the proper URL. Here are the steps to do this:

1. Add the `spring-test` and `hamcrest-all` Maven dependencies in `pom.xml`:

    ```
    <dependency>
        <groupId>org.springframework</groupId>
        <artifactId>spring-test</artifactId>
        <version>4.1.1.RELEASE</version>
        <scope>test</scope>
    </dependency>
    <dependency>
        <groupId>org.hamcrest</groupId>
        <artifactId>hamcrest-all</artifactId>
        <version>1.3</version>
        <scope>test</scope>
    </dependency>
    ```

2. Add the `@WebAppConfiguration` and `@ContextConfiguration` (with the Spring configuration class as a parameter) annotations to the test class:

    ```
    @ContextConfiguration(classes = {AppConfig.class})
    @WebAppConfiguration
    public class StringControllerTest {
    ...
    ```

3. In the test class, add a `WebApplicationContext` attribute:

    ```
    @Autowired
    private WebApplicationContext wac;
    ```

4. In the test class, add a `MockMvc` attribute and initialize it in a `setup()` method using the `WebApplicationContext` attribute:

    ```
    private MockMvc mockMvc;

    @BeforeMethod
    public void setup() {
        this.mockMvc =
    MockMvcBuilders.webAppContextSetup(this.wac).build();
    }
    ```

If you are using JUnit, use the `@Before` annotation.

5. Add these `static` imports to the test class:

```
import static
org.springframework.test.web.servlet.request.
MockMvcRequestBuilders.*;
import static
org.springframework.test.web.servlet.result.
MockMvcResultMatchers.*;
```

6. In the test method, we will build a POST request with the parameters a and b, execute that request, and test whether the web application responds to that URL, if the proper `String` is set in the model, and whether the right JSP is used:

```
@Test
public void testTest1() throws Exception {
    this.mockMvc.perform(post("/concat").param("a",
"red").param("b", "apple"))
    .andExpect(status().isOk())
    .andExpect(model().attribute("result", "redapple"))
    .andExpect(forwardedUrl("/WEB-INF/jsp/concat.jsp"));
}
```

How it works...

The `setup()` method is executed before each test method is executed.

In the `setup()` method, `MockMvcBuilders.webAppContextSetup` performs a full initialization of the controllers and their dependencies, allowing `this.mockMvc.perform()` to retrieve the right controller for a given URL.

There's more...

For debugging, use `andDo(MockMvcResultHandlers.print())` to print the detailed information about the request and the response:

```
this.mockMvc.perform(...)
    ...
        .andDo(MockMvcResultHandlers.print());
```

The output for this recipe looks like:

```
MockHttpServletRequest:
         HTTP Method = POST
         Request URI = /concat
          Parameters = {a=[red], b=[apple]}
             Headers = {}

             Handler:
                Type =
com.spring_cookbook.controllers.StringController
              Method = public java.lang.String
com.spring_cookbook.controllers.StringController.concat
(java.lang.String,java.lang.String,org.springframework.ui.Model)

               Async:
  Was async started = false
        Async result = null

  Resolved Exception:
                Type = null

         ModelAndView:
           View name = concat
                View = null
           Attribute = result
               value = redapple

             FlashMap:

MockHttpServletResponse:
              Status = 200
       Error message = null
             Headers = {}
        Content type = null
                Body =
       Forwarded URL = /WEB-INF/jsp/concat.jsp
      Redirected URL = null
             Cookies = []
```

Explore the `MockMvcRequestBuilders` class to find more elements that can be tested at `http://docs.spring.io/spring/docs/current/javadoc-api/org/springframework/test/web/servlet/request/MockMvcRequestBuilders.html`.

For example, you can test that a GET request gets some JSON content as response, and check the value of a specific element of the response.

```
this.mockMvc.perform(get("/user/5"))
    .andExpect(content().contentType("application/json"))
    .andExpect(jsonPath("$.firstName").value("Scott."));
```

8
Running Batch Jobs

In this chapter, we will cover the following recipes:

- ▶ Installing and configuring Spring Batch
- ▶ Creating a job
- ▶ Executing a job from the command line
- ▶ Executing a job from a controller method
- ▶ Using job parameters
- ▶ Executing a system command
- ▶ Scheduling a job
- ▶ Creating a read/process/write step
- ▶ Reading an XML file
- ▶ Generating a CSV file
- ▶ Reading from a database
- ▶ Unit testing batch jobs

Introduction

A **batch job** is a task executed outside the normal web application workflow (receiving an HTTP request and sending back an HTTP response). It can be executed by the web server as a separate process. It can also be launched directly from the command line.

Typically, a batch job either:

- Imports or exports data at a scheduled time. For example, importing a CSV file in the database every night.

- Executes some code asynchronously to avoid long page loads. For example, processing a video uploaded by the user or generating a big file that will be downloaded by the user.

Spring Batch provides a structure to define, run, and monitor batch jobs. A **Job** is defined as a sequence of steps:

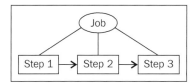

A **Job Instance** is the combination of a **job** and some **parameters**. For example, the day's date and the name of the file to process. A **Job Execution** is created for a job instance. If the job execution fails, another job execution can be created for the same job instance.

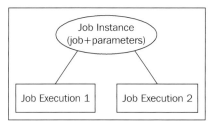

A **Job Execution** generates a **Step Execution** for each step of the job. If a step execution fails, another step execution can be created for that same step:

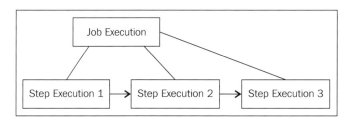

Installing and configuring Spring Batch

Spring automatically saves some metadata (start time, end time, and status) about jobs and their steps in a job repository, which consists of several database tables. In this recipe, we'll create these tables. We will also create a Spring configuration class dedicated to batch jobs.

How to do it...

Here are the steps to install and configure Spring Batch:

1. Add the Maven dependencies for Spring Batch in `pom.xml`:

```
<dependency>
    <groupId>org.springframework.batch</groupId>
    <artifactId>spring-batch-core</artifactId>
    <version>3.0.2.RELEASE</version>
</dependency>

<dependency>
    <groupId>org.springframework.batch</groupId>
    <artifactId>spring-batch-infrastructure</artifactId>
    <version>3.0.2.RELEASE</version>
</dependency>
```

2. Add the Maven dependencies for Spring JDBC and Spring Transaction in `pom.xml`:

```
<dependency>
    <groupId>org.springframework</groupId>
    <artifactId>spring-jdbc</artifactId>
    <version>4.1.2.RELEASE</version>
</dependency>

<dependency>
    <groupId>org.springframework</groupId>
    <artifactId>spring-tx</artifactId>
    <version>4.1.2.RELEASE</version>
</dependency>
```

3. Add the Maven dependency for your database in `pom.xml`:

```
<dependency>
    <groupId>mysql</groupId>
    <artifactId>mysql-connector-java</artifactId>
    <version>5.1.34</version>
</dependency>
```

4. In the database, create the tables for Spring Batch's job repository. The SQL code can be found inside the spring-batch-core dependency in the `org.springframework.batch.core` package. It's also available online at `https://github.com/spring-projects/spring-batch/tree/master/spring-batch-core/src/main/resources/org/springframework/batch/core`.

5. Create a Java package for your Spring Batch classes. For example, `com.spring_cookbook.batch`.

6. Create a Spring configuration class for Spring Batch with the `@EnableBatchProcessing` annotation:

```
@Configuration
@EnableBatchProcessing
public class BatchConfig {
...
}
```

7. Add a `DataSource` bean with the database connection details to the configuration class:

```
@Bean
public DataSource dataSource() {
        DriverManagerDataSource dataSource = new
DriverManagerDataSource();

dataSource.setDriverClassName("com.mysql.jdbc.Driver");
dataSource.setUrl("jdbc:mysql://localhost:3306/db1");
        dataSource.setUsername("root");
        dataSource.setPassword("123");

        return dataSource;
}
```

How it works...

In the configuration class, the `@EnableBatchProcessing` annotation enables Spring Batch and provides reasonable defaults for batch jobs, which can be overridden if necessary (the default `JobLauncher` object, the default `TransactionManager` object, and so on).

Creating a job

We'll create a job that will simply execute some Java code. It will be a job with only one step. The step will be a `Tasklet` object (a single task, as opposed to a read-process-write step, which we'll cover later). We will execute this job in two different ways in the next two recipes.

How to do it...

Create a `Tasklet` class, which you will use to define a step and the job:

1. Create the `Task1` class implementing `Tasklet`:

```
public class Task1 implements Tasklet {


}
```

2. In the `Task1` class, add an `execute()` method with the code to be executed for the job:

```
public RepeatStatus execute(StepContribution contribution,
ChunkContext chunkContext)
        throws Exception {
    System.out.println("Starting job..");

    // ... your code

    System.out.println("Job done..");
    return RepeatStatus.FINISHED;
}
```

3. In the configuration class, add an autowired `JobBuilderFactory` attribute and an autowired `StepBuilderFactory` attribute:

```
@Autowired
private JobBuilderFactory jobs;

@Autowired
private StepBuilderFactory steps;
```

4. Define the `step1` bean, which will execute our code, from the `Task1` class:

```
@Bean
public Step step1(){
    return steps.get("step1")
            .tasklet(new Task1())
            .build();
}
```

5. Define the `job1` bean that will execute `step1`:

```
@Bean
public Job job1(){
    return jobs.get("job1")
            .start(step1())
            .build();
}
```

How it works...

We defined a `job1` job executing the `step1` step, which will call the `execute()` method in the `Task1` class.

There's more...

To execute more than one step, use the `next()` method in the job definition:

```
@Bean
public Job job1(){
    return jobs.get("job1")
            .start(step1())
            .next(step2())
            .build();
}
```

Executing a job from the command line

A simple and robust way to execute a job is to use the command-line interface. This allows you to use a standard `cron` job (use the `AT` command on Windows) to schedule it, so that the job will be executed even if the web application is down. It's also convenient for testing and debugging a job.

Getting Ready

We'll use the job defined in the *Creating a job* recipe.

How to do it...

Follow these steps to execute the job from the command line:

1. Declare the `maven-assembly-plugin` in `pom.xml` (under `build/plugins`):

```
<plugin>
    <artifactId>maven-assembly-plugin</artifactId>
    <configuration>
        <archive>
            <manifest>
                <mainClass>

org.springframework.batch.core.launch.support.
CommandLineJobRunner
                </mainClass>
            </manifest>
        </archive>
        <descriptorRefs>
            <descriptorRef>
jar-with-dependencies</descriptorRef>
        </descriptorRefs>
    </configuration>
</plugin>
```

2. Generate a JAR file:

```
mvn clean compile assembly:single
```

3. Execute the job by running the JAR file generated in the `target` folder, with the class where the job is defined (`BatchConfig`) and the job name (`job1`) as arguments:

```
java -jar target/springwebapp-jar-with-dependencies.jar
com.spring_cookbook.batch.BatchConfig job1
```

4. The console output should look like this:

```
. . .
INFO: Job: [SimpleJob: [name=job1]] launched with the
following parameters: [{}]
. . .
INFO: Executing step: [step1]
Starting job..
Job done..
. . .
```

```
INFO: Job: [SimpleJob: [name=job1]] completed with the following
parameters: [{}] and the following status: [COMPLETED]
...
```

There's more...

A job can be executed only once for a given set of parameters. To be able to execute the job again, just add a parameter using the parameterName=parameterValue syntax:

```
java -jar target/springwebapp-jar-with-dependencies.jar
com.spring_cookbook.batch.BatchConfig job1 p=1
java -jar target/springwebapp-jar-with-dependencies.jar
com.spring_cookbook.batch.BatchConfig job1 p=2
java -jar target/springwebapp-jar-with-dependencies.jar
com.spring_cookbook.batch.BatchConfig job1 p=3
```

In this case, the console output will look like this:

```
...
INFO: Job: [SimpleJob: [name=job1]] launched with the following
parameters: [{p=3}]
...
```

When testing and debugging the job, you can use a Unix timestamp to automatically get a different parameter value each time:

```
java -jar target/springwebapp-jar-with-dependencies.jar
com.spring_cookbook.batch.BatchConfig job1 p=`date +'%s'`
```

A job can be also be executed directly without having to generate a JAR file first:

```
mvn compile exec:java -
Dexec.mainClass=org.springframework.batch.core.launch.support.
CommandLineJobRunner -
Dexec.args="com.spring_cookbook.batch.BatchConfig job1 p=4"
```

Executing a job from a controller method

It's convenient to launch a job from a controller method when that job is triggered by a user action. For example, launching a job to process a video just uploaded by the user.

Getting ready

We'll use the job defined in the *Creating a job* recipe.

How to do it...

Follow these steps to execute the job from a controller method:

1. Add the Spring Batch configuration class to the `getServletConfigClasses()` method in your class extending `AbstractAnnotationConfigDispatcherServletInitializer`:

   ```
   public class ServletInitializer extends
   AbstractAnnotationConfigDispatcherServletInitializer {

   @Override
   protected Class<?>[] getServletConfigClasses() {
       return new Class<?>[]{AppConfig.class,
   BatchConfig.class};
   }
   ```

2. In your controller class, add a `JobLauncher` attribute and `Job` attribute both autowired:

   ```
   @Autowired
   JobLauncher jobLauncher;

   @Autowired
   Job job;
   ```

3. In the controller method, define the job parameters and launch the job:

   ```
   try {
      JobParametersBuilder jobParametersBuilder = new
   JobParametersBuilder();
      jobParametersBuilder.addDate("d", new Date());

      jobLauncher.run(job,
   jobParametersBuilder.toJobParameters());
   } catch (Exception e) {
      ...
   }
   ```

How it works...

We declared `BatchConfig` in the `ServletInitializer` class to make our Spring Batch configuration available to the controller methods.

In the controller method, the job parameters are the same as those in the command line.

Using job parameters

In this recipe, you'll learn how to retrieve and use a job parameter value in `Tasklet`.

Getting ready

We'll use the job defined in the *Creating a job* recipe.

How to do it...

Follow these steps to use the job parameters:

1. In the `Task1` class, add `@StepScope` to the `execute()` method:

    ```
    @StepScope
    public RepeatStatus execute(StepContribution contribution,
    ChunkContext chunkContext)
            throws Exception {
    . . .
    ```

2. In the `execute()` method, retrieve a job parameter value by using the job parameter name:

    ```
    String test =
    (String)chunkContext.getStepContext().getJobParameters().
    get("test")
    ```

3. Run the job with a parameter named `test`:

    ```
    mvn compile exec:java -
    Dexec.mainClass=org.springframework.batch.core.launch.
    support.CommandLineJobRunner -
    Dexec.args="com.spring_cookbook.batch.BatchConfig job1
    test=hello"
    ```

How it works...

The `String` test will contain the `hello` parameter value passed on the command line. This recipe will also work if the job is launched from a controller method.

Executing a system command

A step can consist of just an execution of a system command. Spring Batch provides a convenient class for this, `SystemCommandTasklet`.

Getting ready

We'll use the job defined in the *Creating a job* recipe.

How to do it...

In Spring Batch's configuration file, add a `SystemCommandTasklet` bean. Declare the system command to be executed (here, we used the touch Unix command to create an empty file), the directory to execute it from, and the maximum time allowed for its execution:

```
@Bean
public SystemCommandTasklet task1() {
  SystemCommandTasklet tasklet = new
SystemCommandTasklet();

  tasklet.setCommand("touch test.txt");
  tasklet.setWorkingDirectory("/home/merlin");
  tasklet.setTimeout(5000);

  return tasklet;
}
```

How it works...

The `SystemCommandTasklet` class will execute a command from the working directory and kill the process if it exceeds the timeout value.

There's more...

For a more advanced use of system commands (for example, to get the output of the system command) extend `SystemCommandTasklet` and override its `execute()` method.

Scheduling a job

Some jobs need to be executed regularly-every night, every hour, and so on. Spring makes this easy with the `@Scheduled` annotation.

Getting ready

We will use the job defined in the *Creating a job* recipe.

How to do it...

Follow these steps to schedule the job:

1. If it's not done already, add the Spring Batch configuration class to the `getServletConfigClasses()` method in your class extending `AbstractAnnotationConfigDispatcherServletInitializer`:

   ```
   public class ServletInitializer extends
   AbstractAnnotationConfigDispatcherServletInitializer {

   @Override
   protected Class<?>[] getServletConfigClasses() {
       return new Class<?>[]{AppConfig.class,
   BatchConfig.class};
   }
   ```

2. Add the `@EnableScheduling` annotation to the Spring Batch configuration class:

   ```
   @Configuration
   @EnableBatchProcessing
   @EnableScheduling
   public class BatchConfig {
   ...
   ```

3. Add an autowired `JobLauncher` field:

   ```
   @Autowired
   JobLauncher jobLauncher;
   ```

4. Add a method annotated with `@Scheduled` with a `fixedDelay` attribute in ms:

   ```
   @Scheduled(fixedDelay=10000)
   public void runJob1() throws Exception {
   ...
   }
   ```

5. In that method, run the job:

   ```
   JobParametersBuilder jobParametersBuilder = new
   JobParametersBuilder();
   jobParametersBuilder.addDate("d", new Date());
   jobLauncher.run(job1(),
   jobParametersBuilder.toJobParameters());
   ```

How it works...

The job will start getting executed again and again with a 10-second (10000 ms) interval as soon as the web application is deployed. The `job` parameter with the `new Date()` value is used to set a different parameter value for each launch.

There's more...

The `fixedDelay` attribute sets a delay of 10 seconds after a job has finished its execution before launching the next one. To actually run a job every 10 seconds, use `fixedRate`:

```
@Scheduled(fixedRate=10000)
public void runJob1() throws Exception {
...
}
```

It's also possible to use a regular `cron` expression:

```
@Scheduled(cron="*/5 * * * *")
public void runJob1() throws Exception {
...
}
```

Creating a read/process/write step

A read/process/write step is a common type of step where some data is read somewhere, processed in some way, and finally, saved somewhere else. In this recipe, we'll read a CSV file of users, increment their age, and save the modified users in a database as shown in the following image:

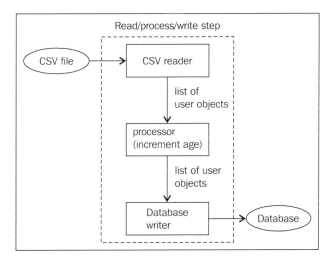

Getting ready

This is our CSV file of users, `input_data.txt`:

```
Merlin, 333
Arthur, 37
Lancelot, 35
Tristan, 20
Iseult, 22
Mark, 56
```

For each line of the CSV file, we'll create a `User` object. So, make sure that the `User` class exists:

```
public class User {
  private String firstName;
  private int age;
...
}
```

Each `User` object will be saved in the database. Make sure that the `user` table exists:

```
CREATE TABLE user  (
    id BIGINT NOT NULL PRIMARY KEY AUTO_INCREMENT,
  first_name TEXT,
  age INT
);
```

How to do it...

Follow these steps to process the CSV file:

1. In the Spring Batch configuration class, add a method returning a `LineMapper` object, which generates an `User` object from a line in the CSV file:

```
private LineMapper<User> lineMapper() {
  DefaultLineMapper<User> lineMapper = new
DefaultLineMapper<User>();

  DelimitedLineTokenizer lineTokenizer = new
DelimitedLineTokenizer();
    lineTokenizer.setNames(new
String[]{"firstName","age"});
    lineTokenizer.setIncludedFields(new int[]{0,1});
    lineMapper.setLineTokenizer(lineTokenizer);
```

```
        BeanWrapperFieldSetMapper<User> fieldSetMapper = new
    BeanWrapperFieldSetMapper<User>();
        fieldSetMapper.setTargetType(User.class);
        lineMapper.setFieldSetMapper(fieldSetMapper);

        return lineMapper;
    }
```

2. Add a `reader()` method returning a `FlatFileItemReader` object, which will read a CSV file (whose path is the file path of the CSV file), and use the previously defined `LineMapper` object to generate users:

```
@Bean
@StepScope
public FlatFileItemReader<User>
reader(@Value("#{jobParameters[file]}") String csvFilePath)
{
    FlatFileItemReader<User> reader = new
FlatFileItemReader<User>();
    reader.setLineMapper(lineMapper());
    reader.setResource(new PathResource(csvFilePath));

    reader.setLinesToSkip(1);
    reader.setEncoding("utf-8");

    return reader;
}
```

3. Define a class implementing `ItemProcessor` with a `process()` method that takes a `User` object, increments its `age`, and returns the modified `User` object:

```
public class UserProcessorIncrementAge implements
ItemProcessor<User, User> {

    public User process(User user) throws Exception {
        int age = user.getAge();
        age++;
        user.setAge(age);
        return user;
    }

}
```

4. Back in the Batch configuration class, define a `UserProcessorIncrementAge` bean:

```
@Bean
private ItemProcessor<User,User> processor() {
    return new UserProcessorIncrementAge();
}
```

5. Define a `Datasource` bean with the database connection details:

```
@Bean
public DataSource dataSource() {
  DriverManagerDataSource dataSource = new
DriverManagerDataSource();

    dataSource.setDriverClassName("com.mysql.jdbc.Driver");
    dataSource.setUrl("jdbc:mysql://localhost:3306/db1");
    dataSource.setUsername("root");
    dataSource.setPassword("123");

    return dataSource;
}
```

6. Add a `writer()` bean that will take a `User` object and save it in the database:

```
@Bean
public JdbcBatchItemWriter<User> writer(){
    JdbcBatchItemWriter<User> writer = new
JdbcBatchItemWriter<User>();
    writer.setDataSource(dataSource());
    writer.setSql("INSERT INTO user (first_name, age) " +
        "VALUES ( :firstName, :age)");
    ItemSqlParameterSourceProvider<User> paramProvider =
new BeanPropertyItemSqlParameterSourceProvider<User>();

    writer.setItemSqlParameterSourceProvider(paramProvider);
    return writer;
}
```

7. Add a `JobBuilderFactory` field and a `StepBuilderFactory` field, both autowired:

```
@Autowired
private JobBuilderFactory jobs;

@Autowired
private StepBuilderFactory steps;
```

8. Define a step calling our `reader()`, `processor()`, and `writer()` methods:

```
@Bean
public Step step1(){
    return steps.get("step")
            .<User,User>chunk(1)
            .reader(reader(null))
            .processor(processor())
            .writer(writer())
            .build();
}
```

9. Define a job with the previous defined step:

```
@Bean
public Job job1(){
    return jobs.get("job1")
            .start(step1())
            .build();
}
```

10. Execute the job with the path to the CSV file as parameter:

```
mvn compile exec:java -
Dexec.mainClass=org.springframework.batch.core.launch.
support.CommandLineJobRunner -
Dexec.args="com.spring_cookbook.batch.BatchConfig job1
file=input_data.txt"
```

How it works...

In the `reader()` method, we used `FlatFileItemReader`, which is a class provided by Spring Batch for reading CSV files. Each line is processed by `LineMapper`, which takes a line and returns an object. In this recipe, we used `DefaultLineMapper`, which converts a line to `Fieldset` (using `DelimitedLineTokenizer`) and then saves each field in an object (all of this is done behind the scenes by `BeanWrapperFieldSetMapper`).

In the `writer()` method, we supplied the SQL query, which will create the user in the database. The values come automatically from the `User` object, thanks to the `BeanPropertyItemSqlParameterSourceProvider` class. For example, `:firstName` will get its value from the `User` object's `firstName` field.

In the `step1()` method, we declared the reader, processor, and writer methods. The `chunk()` method allows the data to be processed and saved by groups (in chunks). This is more efficient for large sets of data.

The `@StepScope` annotation is necessary for the `reader()` and `writer()` methods, to allow them to access the job parameters. Otherwise, they are executed too early in the job initialization process.

There's more...

The reader-processor-writer separation makes it easy to swap one component with another. For example, if our CSV file becomes an XML file one day, we will only have to update the `reader()` method. In the next recipes, we will cover other types of readers and writers.

A processor is not required in a read/process/write job, so skip it if you don't need it. It also doesn't need to return an object from the same class. For example, it could take a `UserCSV` object, which would be a direct mapping of a line of the CSV file and return an actual `User` object. This would allow you to keep the CSV reader straightforward and separate the code converting its data to an actual `User` object, your real domain object, making that code easier to understand and maintain.

Our reader and writer code is short enough, so we will put it directly in the Spring Batch configuration. However, it could be moved to separate classes.

Reading an XML file

In this recipe, you'll learn to read an XML file as part of a read/process/write step.

Getting ready

We'll read this XML file:

```xml
<?xml version="1.0" encoding="UTF-8"?>
<records>
    <person>
        <firstName>Shania</firstName>
    <age>49</age>
    </person>
    <person>
        <firstName>Nelly</firstName>
    <age>36</age>
    </person>
</records>
```

For each person's record in the XML file, a `User` object will be created. Make sure that the `User` class exists:

```
public class User {
  private String firstName;
  private int age;
```

How to do it...

To parse the XML file, use `StaxEventItemReader`, which is provided by Spring Batch. To generate `User` objects, use `XStreamMarshaller`, a class from the Spring Object/XML Mapping project. Follow these steps:

1. Add the Maven dependency for Spring Object/XML Mapping in `pom.xml`:

    ```
    <dependency>
      <groupId>org.springframework</groupId>
      <artifactId>spring-oxm</artifactId>
      <version>${spring.version}</version>
    </dependency>
    ```

2. Add a `reader()` method returning a `StaxEventItemReader` object to read the XML file and generate `User` objects from its contents:

    ```
    @Bean
    @StepScope
    public StaxEventItemReader<User>
    reader(@Value("#{jobParameters[file]}") String xmlFilePath)
    {
        StaxEventItemReader<User> reader = new
    StaxEventItemReader<User>();
        reader.setResource(new PathResource(xmlFilePath));
        reader.setFragmentRootElementName("person");

      XStreamMarshaller marshaller = new XStreamMarshaller();
      marshaller.setAliases(Collections.singletonMap("person",
    User.class));
        reader.setUnmarshaller(marshaller);

        return reader;
    }
    ```

3. Execute the job with the path to the XML file as a parameter. For example:

```
mvn compile exec:java -
Dexec.mainClass=org.springframework.batch.core.launch.
support.CommandLineJobRunner -
Dexec.args="com.spring_cookbook.batch.BatchConfig job1
file=input_data.xml
```

How it works...

XStreamMarshaller generates a User automatically for each person's record. This is configured with the following line:

```
marshaller.setAliases(Collections.singletonMap("person",
User.class));
```

Note that the User fields have to match the XML fields (firstName and age).

Generating a CSV file

Write a CSV file as part of a read/process/write step.

Getting ready

We will generate a CSV file from User objects. Make sure that the User class exists:

```
public class User {
  private String firstName;
  private int age;
```

How to do it...

Use FlatFileItemWriter provided by Spring Batch:

1. Add a writer() method that will get the fields of a User object, build a comma-separated line with them, and write the line to a CSV file:

```
@Bean
@StepScope
public FlatFileItemWriter<User>
writer(@Value("#{jobParameters[fileOut]}") String
csvFilePath) {
    BeanWrapperFieldExtractor<User> fieldExtractor = new
BeanWrapperFieldExtractor<User>();
```

```
        fieldExtractor.setNames(new
    String[]{"firstName","age"});

        DelimitedLineAggregator<User> lineAggregator = new
    DelimitedLineAggregator<User>();
        lineAggregator.setDelimiter(",");
        lineAggregator.setFieldExtractor(fieldExtractor);

        FlatFileItemWriter<User> writer = new
    FlatFileItemWriter<User>();
        writer.setLineAggregator(lineAggregator);
        writer.setResource(new PathResource(csvFilePath));

        return writer;
    }
```

2. Execute the job with the path to the output CSV file as a parameter:

```
mvn compile exec:java -
Dexec.mainClass=org.springframework.batch.core.launch.
support.CommandLineJobRunner -
Dexec.args="com.spring_cookbook.batch.BatchConfig job1
file=input_data.txt fileOut=output_data.txt
```

3. The resulting CSV file will look like this:

```
Merlin,334
Arthur,38
Lancelot,36
Tristan,21
Iseult,23
Mark,57
```

How it works...

BeanWrapperFieldExtractor extracts the declared fields (firstName and age) from the User object. DelimitedLineAggregator builds a comma-separated line with them. FlatFileItemWriter writes the line to the file.

Reading from a database

This recipe shows you how to read data from a database as part of a read/process/write step.

Getting ready

Each user will be read from the database. Make sure that the `user` database table exists with some data in it:

```
CREATE TABLE user  (
    id BIGINT NOT NULL PRIMARY KEY AUTO_INCREMENT,
  first_name TEXT,
  age INT
);
```

For each user row in the database, we'll create a `User` object. Make sure that the `User` class exists:

```
public class User {
   private String firstName;
   private int age;
```

Make sure that the `Datasource` bean is defined with the database connection information.

How to do it...

Add a `reader()` method returning `JdbcCursorItemReader`-a class provided by Spring Batch:

```
@Bean
@StepScope
public JdbcCursorItemReader<User> reader() {
  JdbcCursorItemReader<User> reader = new
JdbcCursorItemReader<User>();
  reader.setDataSource(dataSource());

  reader.setSql("SELECT first_name, age FROM user");

  reader.setRowMapper(new
BeanPropertyRowMapper<User>(User.class));

  return reader;
}
```

How it works...

A SQL query is executed to get users from the database. `BeanPropertyRowMapper` generates `User` objects from the result. Note that the SQL result's columns (`first_name`, `age`) have to match the User fields (`firstName` and `age`). If the database table has different column names, use SQL aliases to ensure that:

```
SELECT name1 as first_name, the_age as age FROM user
```

Unit testing batch jobs

Spring Batch provides different ways to test a batch job; the whole job, only one step, or just a `Tasklet` class can be tested.

How to do it...

Follow these steps to unit test batch jobs:

1. Add the Maven dependency for `spring-batch-test` in `pom.xml`:

    ```
    <dependency>
      <groupId>org.springframework.batch</groupId>
      <artifactId>spring-batch-test</artifactId>
      <version>3.0.2.RELEASE</version>
    </dependency>
    ```

2. In the unit test class, if using JUnit, load the Spring Batch configuration class like this:

    ```
    @RunWith(SpringJUnit4ClassRunner.class)
    @ContextConfiguration(classes = {BatchConfig.class})
    public class BatchJob1Test {
    ...
    ```

3. If using TestNG, load the Spring Batch configuration class as follows:

    ```
    @ContextConfiguration(classes = {BatchConfig.class})
    public class BatchJob1Test extends
    AbstractTestNGSpringContextTests {
    ...
    ```

4. Add an autowired `JobLauncherTestUtils` field:

    ```
    @Autowired
    private JobLauncherTestUtils jobLauncherTestUtils;
    ```

5. This is how you can test an entire job, check its exit status, and the number of steps that were executed:

```
@Test
public void testJob() throws Exception {
    JobExecution jobExecution =
jobLauncherTestUtils.launchJob();
    Assert.assertEquals(ExitStatus.COMPLETED,
jobExecution.getExitStatus());
    Assert.assertEquals(1,
jobExecution.getStepExecutions().size());
}
```

6. This is how you can test a specific step:

```
@Test
public void testStep() throws Exception {
    JobExecution jobExecution =
jobLauncherTestUtils.launchStep("step1");
    Assert.assertEquals(ExitStatus.COMPLETED,
jobExecution.getExitStatus());
}
```

7. This is how you can test Tasklet:

```
@Test
public void testTasklet() throws Exception {
    Task1 task1 = new Task1();
    Assert.assertEquals(RepeatStatus.FINISHED,
task1.execute(null, null));
}
```

How it works...

The Spring Batch configuration class has to be loaded, so that the test methods can access the job and its steps. `JobLauncherTestUtils` is a helper class that is used to easily execute a job or one of its steps.

9
Handling Mobiles and Tablets

In this chapter, we will cover the following recipes:

- ▶ Installing Spring Mobile
- ▶ Detecting mobiles and tablets
- ▶ Switching to the normal view on mobiles
- ▶ Using different JSP views for mobiles automatically
- ▶ Using a `.mobi` domain name on mobiles
- ▶ Using an `m.` subdomain on mobiles
- ▶ Using a different domain name on mobiles
- ▶ Using a subfolder path on mobiles

Introduction

To build a mobile-friendly website, the current trend is to use responsive design where the page adapts to the screen width. This way, the same page is nicely displayed on all devices: computers, tablets and mobiles.

Another approach, which this chapter covers, is to build a separate website for mobile devices. This requires building two pages (different HTML and distinct URLs) for each page of the website: one for the computer and one for the mobile. This extra work makes sense when:

▸ Performance is important. For example, the loading time of a responsive website like `https://www.flickr.com/` would be too long on mobile devices because of the high-resolution images of the desktop version. A separate mobile website makes it easier to optimize the user experience on mobile devices.

▸ The computer version of the website already exists; in this case, it's usually much simpler to build a separate mobile website.

In this chapter, we'll cover how to serve different pages to mobile devices using Spring Mobile, a Spring project.

Installing Spring Mobile

In this recipe, you'll learn how to install Spring Mobile and prepare the Spring configuration class for the other recipes.

How to do it...

Here are the steps to install Spring Mobile:

1. Add the Maven dependency for Spring Mobile in `pom.xml`:

```
<dependency>
  <groupId>org.springframework.mobile</groupId>
  <artifactId>spring-mobile-device</artifactId>
  <version>1.1.3.RELEASE</version>
</dependency>
```

2. Make the Spring configuration class extend `WebMvcConfigurerAdapter`:

```
@Configuration
@EnableWebMvc
@ComponentScan(basePackages =
{"com.spring_cookbook.controllers"})
public class AppConfig extends WebMvcConfigurerAdapter {
```

3. Override the `addInterceptors()` method from `WebMvcConfigurerAdapter`:

```
@Override
public void addInterceptors(InterceptorRegistry registry) {
}
```

How it works...

The `addInterceptors()` method will be used in the following recipes to register various interceptors.

There's more...

For more information about interceptors, refer to the *Executing some code before and after controllers using interceptors* recipe in *Chapter 3, Using Controllers and Views*.

Detecting mobiles and tablets

In this recipe, you'll learn how, from a controller method, you can detect whether the current HTTP request has come from a desktop computer, mobile, or tablet.

How to do it...

Register a `DeviceResolverHandlerInterceptor` interceptor and use `DeviceUtils` in the controller method:

1. In the Spring configuration class, declare a `DeviceResolverHandlerInterceptor` bean:

```
@Bean
public DeviceResolverHandlerInterceptor
deviceResolverHandlerInterceptor() {
    return new DeviceResolverHandlerInterceptor();
}
```

2. Register the `DeviceResolverHandlerInterceptor` bean as an interceptor in the `addInterceptors()` method:

```
@Override
public void addInterceptors(InterceptorRegistry registry) {
registry.addInterceptor(deviceResolverHandlerInterceptor())
;
}
```

3. Add an `HttpServletRequest` argument to your controller method:

```
@Controller
public class UserController {
  @RequestMapping("/user_list")
  public void userList(HttpServletRequest request) {
```

4. Use `DeviceUtils.getCurrentDevice()` to generate a `Device` object from `HttpServletRequest`:

```
Device currentDevice =
DeviceUtils.getCurrentDevice(request);
```

5. Use the `Device` object to detect the type of device that sent the request:

```
if(currentDevice == null) {
  // detection failed
}
if(currentDevice.isMobile()) {
  // mobile
}
else if(currentDevice.isTablet()) {
  // tablet
}
else if(currentDevice.isNormal()) {
  // desktop computer
}
```

How it works...

The `DeviceResolverHandlerInterceptor` interceptor generates a `Device` object from the HTTP request and stores it in `HttpServletRequest`, passed to the controller method. `DeviceUtils.getCurrentDevice()` is a convenient method to retrieve the `Device` object.

You can then choose to display different JSPs based on the `Device` type.

To generate the `Device` object, `DeviceResolverHandlerInterceptor` uses `LiteDeviceResolver` by default, which uses the **User-Agent** header of the HTTP request. The algorithm is based on WordPress Mobile Pack's detection algorithm.

Switching to the normal view on mobiles

A mobile user gets the mobile version of the website by default, but he/she may want to access some contents displayed only on the normal version. Spring Mobile offers the `SitePreference` object for that purpose, which is to be used instead of the `Device` object used in the previous recipe.

How to do it...

Follow these steps to create links, to switch between the normal version and the mobile version of a website:

1. In the Spring configuration class, declare a DeviceResolverHandlerInterceptor bean and a SitePreferenceHandlerInterceptor bean and register them as interceptors:

```
@Bean
public DeviceResolverHandlerInterceptor
deviceResolverHandlerInterceptor() {
    return new DeviceResolverHandlerInterceptor();
}

@Bean
public SitePreferenceHandlerInterceptor
sitePreferenceHandlerInterceptor() {
    return new SitePreferenceHandlerInterceptor();
}


@Override
public void addInterceptors(InterceptorRegistry registry) {
    registry.addInterceptor(deviceResolverHandlerInterceptor())
;
    registry.addInterceptor(sitePreferenceHandlerInterceptor())
;
}
```

2. In your controller method, add an HttpServletRequest argument:

```
@Controller
public class UserController {
  @RequestMapping("/user_list")
  public void userList(HttpServletRequest request) {
```

3. Use SitePreferenceUtils.getCurrentSitePreference() to generate a SitePreference object:

```
SitePreference sitePreference =
SitePreferenceUtils.getCurrentSitePreference(request);
```

4. Use the `SitePreference` object to detect the version of the page to be displayed:

```
if(sitePreference == null || sitePreference.isNormal()) {
  // normal
}
if(sitePreference.isMobile()) {
  // mobile
}
```

5. In the view, add links to the two versions of the page:

```
Site:
<a href="?site_preference=normal">Normal</a>
|
<a href="?site_preference=mobile">Mobile</a>
```

How it works...

Spring Mobile automatically detects the `site_preference` parameter (via the `SitePreferenceHandlerInterceptor` interceptor) and adjusts the `SitePreference` value accordingly.

By default, the `SitePreference` value is the same as `Device`. For example, a *mobile* preference for a *mobile* device. When the user clicks on a link containing a `site_preference` parameter, the site preference is changed, but the device type remains the same. For example, a *normal* preference for a *mobile* device.

There's more...

Spring Mobile supports a *tablet* site preference. Some websites provide pages optimized for tablets; Google Search, for example, provides a page optimized for tablets.

Using different JSP views for mobiles automatically

Instead of having to manually select the correct JSP in each controller method depending on the request device or site preference, use `LiteDeviceDelegatingViewResolver` provided by Spring Mobile.

How to do it...

In the Spring configuration class, replace any existing `ViewResolver` bean with a `LiteDeviceDelegatingViewResolver` bean:

```
@Bean
public LiteDeviceDelegatingViewResolver
liteDeviceAwareViewResolver() {
    InternalResourceViewResolver delegate = new
InternalResourceViewResolver();
    delegate.setPrefix("/WEB-INF/jsp/");
    delegate.setSuffix(".jsp");
    LiteDeviceDelegatingViewResolver resolver = new
LiteDeviceDelegatingViewResolver(delegate);
    resolver.setMobilePrefix("mobile/");
    resolver.setEnableFallback(true);
    return resolver;
}
```

How it works...

For a controller returning the `userList` String, the `/WEB-INF/userList.jsp` JSP view will be used if the site preference is *normal*. The `/WEB-INF/mobile/userList.jsp` JSP view will be used if the site preference is *mobile*.

If the site preference is *mobile* and `/WEB-INF/mobile/userList.jsp` doesn't exist, `/WEB-INF/userList.jsp` will be used as a fallback instead. This is enabled by the line:

```
resolver.setEnableFallback(true);
```

There's more...

`LiteDeviceDelegatingViewResolver` supports custom JSP views for tablets:

```
resolver.setTabletPrefix("tablet/");
```

Using a .mobi domain name on mobiles

In this recipe, you'll learn how to use a top-level `.mobi` domain name for the mobile pages of your website. For example:

- ► `mysite.com` for the normal website
- ► `mysite.mobi` for the mobile version

The top-level domain name `.mobi` has been created to enable visitors of a website to ask explicitly for its mobile version. For example, http://google.mobi. Google, Microsoft, Nokia, and Samsung originally sponsored it.

Getting ready

Make sure that the `SitePreferenceHandlerInterceptor` interceptor is declared in the Spring configuration. Refer to the *Switching to the normal view on mobiles* recipe in this chapter.

How to do it...

Follow these steps to use a `.mobi` domain name for the mobile version of the website:

1. In the Spring configuration, declare a `SiteSwitcherHandlerInterceptor` bean initialized with the `dotMobi()` method with your main domain name as a parameter:

    ```
    @Bean
    public SiteSwitcherHandlerInterceptor
    siteSwitcherHandlerInterceptor() {
        return
    SiteSwitcherHandlerInterceptor.dotMobi("mywebsite.com");
    }
    ```

2. Declare that bean as an interceptor:

    ```
    @Override
    public void addInterceptors(InterceptorRegistry registry) {
        ...
    registry.addInterceptor(siteSwitcherHandlerInterceptor());
    }
    ```

How it works...

Behind the scenes, `SiteSwitcherHandlerInterceptor` reads the current `SitePreference` value (*normal*, *tablet*, or *mobile*) and performs a redirect to the correct domain name if necessary. For example, an HTTP request from a mobile device for `mywebsite.com` will be automatically redirected to `mywebsite.mobi`. A tablet will go to the normal website.

Using an m. subdomain on mobiles

In this recipe, you'll learn how to use an `m.` subdomain for the mobile pages of your website. For example:

- `mysite.com` for the normal website
- `m.mysite.com` for the mobile version

Some advantages of an `m.` subdomain are:

- No need to purchase another domain name (and another SSL certificate if you're using HTTPS)
- It is easy to remember for the user

Getting ready

Make sure that the `SitePreferenceHandlerInterceptor` interceptor is declared in the Spring configuration. Refer to the *Switching to the normal view on mobiles* recipe in this chapter.

How to do it...

Follow these steps to use a `m.` subdomain for the mobile version of the website:

1. In the Spring configuration, declare a `SiteSwitcherHandlerInterceptor` bean initialized with the `mDot()` method with your main domain name as a parameter:

   ```
   @Bean
   public SiteSwitcherHandlerInterceptor
   siteSwitcherHandlerInterceptor() {
       return
   SiteSwitcherHandlerInterceptor.mDot("mywebsite.com");
   }
   ```

2. Declare that bean as an interceptor:

   ```
   @Override
   public void addInterceptors(InterceptorRegistry registry) {
       ...
   registry.addInterceptor(siteSwitcherHandlerInterceptor());
   }
   ```

How it works...

Behind the scenes, `SiteSwitcherHandlerInterceptor` reads the current `SitePreference` value (*normal*, *tablet*, or *mobile*) and performs a redirect to the correct domain name if necessary. For example, an HTTP request from a mobile device for `mywebsite.com` will be automatically redirected to `m.mywebsite.com`. A tablet will go to the normal website.

Using a different domain name on mobiles

In this recipe, you'll learn how to use a different domain name for the mobile pages of your website. For example:

- `mysite.com` for the normal website
- `mymobilesite.com` for the mobile version

Getting ready

Make sure that the `SitePreferenceHandlerInterceptor` interceptor is declared in the Spring configuration. Refer to the *Switching to the normal view on mobiles* recipe in this chapter.

How to do it...

Follow these steps to use a different domain name for the mobile version of the website:

1. In the Spring configuration, declare a `SiteSwitcherHandlerInterceptor` bean initialized with the `standard()` method with your main domain name, mobile domain name, and the value for the `Set-Cookie` HTTP header field:

```
@Bean
public SiteSwitcherHandlerInterceptor
siteSwitcherHandlerInterceptor() {
    return
SiteSwitcherHandlerInterceptor.standard("mywebsite.com",
"mymobilewebsite.com", ".mywebsite.com");
}
```

2. Declare that bean as an interceptor:

```
@Override
public void addInterceptors(InterceptorRegistry registry) {
    ...
    registry.addInterceptor(siteSwitcherHandlerInterceptor());
}
```

How it works...

Behind the scenes, `SiteSwitcherHandlerInterceptor` reads the current `SitePreference` value (*normal*, *tablet*, or *mobile*) and performs a redirect to the correct domain name if necessary. For example, an HTTP request from a mobile device for `mywebsite.com` will be redirected automatically to `mymobilewebsite.com`. A tablet will go to the normal website.

The `Set-Cookie` HTTP header field contains the `SitePreference` value. The cookie allows us to share that value with subdomains. In this recipe, `.mywebsite.com` makes the `SitePreference` value available to `www.mywebsite.com`, for example.

Using a subfolder path on mobiles

In this recipe, you'll learn how to use a subfolder in the URL for the mobile pages of your website. For example:

- ▶ `mysite.com` for the normal website
- ▶ `mysite.com/mobile` for the mobile version

Getting ready

Make sure that the `SitePreferenceHandlerInterceptor` interceptor is declared in the Spring configuration. Refer to the *Switching to the normal view on mobiles* recipe in this chapter.

How to do it...

Follow these steps to use a subfolder path for the mobile version of the website:

1. In the Spring configuration, declare a `SiteSwitcherHandlerInterceptor` bean initialized with the `urlPath()` method with the subfolder name and the web application root path if necessary:

```
@Bean
public SiteSwitcherHandlerInterceptor
siteSwitcherHandlerInterceptor() {
    return SiteSwitcherHandlerInterceptor.urlPath("/mobile",
"spring_webapp");
}
```

2. Declare that bean as an interceptor:

```
@Override
public void addInterceptors(InterceptorRegistry registry) {
   ...
   registry.addInterceptor(siteSwitcherHandlerInterceptor());
}
```

3. Add the controller method for the URL with the `mobile` subfolder:

```
@RequestMapping("/mobile/user_list")
public String userListMobile(HttpServletRequest request) {
   ...
   return "user_list";
}
```

How it works...

Behind the scenes, `SiteSwitcherHandlerInterceptor` reads the current `SitePreference` value (*normal*, *tablet*, or *mobile*) and performs a redirect to add or remove the `mobile` subfolder to the URL if necessary. For example, an HTTP request from a mobile device for `mywebsite.com` will be automatically redirected to `mywebsite.com/mobile`. A tablet will go to the normal website.

10
Connecting to Facebook and Twitter

In this chapter, we will cover the following recipes:

- ▶ Creating a Facebook app
- ▶ Creating a test Facebook app and test users
- ▶ Connecting to Facebook
- ▶ Retrieving a Facebook user's profile
- ▶ Retrieving the list of friends of a Facebook user
- ▶ Posting a Facebook status update
- ▶ Posting a link to Facebook
- ▶ Posting a custom object to Facebook
- ▶ Creating a Twitter application
- ▶ Connecting to Twitter
- ▶ Retrieving a user's Twitter profile
- ▶ Retrieving the tweets of a Twitter user
- ▶ Posting a tweet to Twitter
- ▶ Sending a private message to another Twitter user

Introduction

In this chapter, we will make a Spring web application access Facebook and Twitter accounts in order to:

- ▶ Retrieve user data, such as name, e-mail, tweets, posts, and so on
- ▶ Create user data, such as a tweet, Facebook post, and so on

For that, we will use Spring Social, which simplifies interacting with social networks from a Spring web application; it helps with the OAuth workflows and executes the proper REST requests behind the scenes for us.

Creating a Facebook app

A web application can access a Facebook account only through a Facebook app. In this recipe, we will open a Facebook developer account and create a Facebook app. We will obtain an **App ID** and **App secret**, which are the two strings that our web application will use to connect to Facebook in the following recipes.

Getting ready

Log in to your Facebook account.

How to do it...

Here are the steps to open a Facebook developer account and create a Facebook app:

1. Go to `https://developers.facebook.com/`.
2. In the top navigation, in **My Apps**, select **Register as a Developer**.
3. Once you're registered, in the top menu, under **Apps**, select **Add a New App**.
4. Select **Website**.

5. Click on **Skip and Create App ID** in the top-right corner of the window:

6. Fill in the form and click on **Create App ID**.

7. Find the **App ID** and **App Secret** displayed on the app page.

Creating a test Facebook app and test users

To work with actual Facebook users, a Facebook app needs to go through an approval process; you have to submit some screenshots, a logo, description, and privacy policy. To just test your web application, skip the approval process by using a **Test App** with **Test Users**. Facebook provides a convenient interface to create them.

Getting ready

You need an existing Facebook app. Refer to the previous *Creating a Facebook app* recipe.

How to do it...

Here are the steps to create a test app and test users:

1. Go to `https://developers.facebook.com/apps`.

2. Select your existing app.

3. In the left side of the navigation menu, select **Test Apps**.

4. Click on the **Create a Test App** green button.

5. Enter a name for your test app and create the app.

6. The test app's **App ID** and **App Secret** are displayed. They are different from the original app. Use them in your Spring web application to use the test app.

7. In the left side of the navigation menu, select **Roles**. Choose the **Test Users** tab and click on the **Add** button.

8. Select **4 users**. Leave the other options to their default value and click on **Create Test Users**.

9. Choose one of the created users, click on the **Edit** button, and choose **Change the name or password for this user**.

10. Choose a password for the user and click on **Save**.

11. Click again on the **Edit** button of the same test user and select **Manage this test user's friends**.

12. Type the names of a few other test users and click on **Save**.

How it works...

We defined a password for one user, so we'll be able to log in as this user and authorize our web application in the following recipes.

We also added friends to that user, so we'll be able to test the *Retrieving the list of friends of a Facebook user* recipe.

Connecting to Facebook

Facebook allows access to a user account through an **OAuth workflow**; from our web application, the user is redirected to a Facebook page to authorize our Facebook app to access his/her account. The user is then redirected back to our web application. In this recipe, we'll implement this OAuth workflow.

Getting ready

You need an existing Facebook app. Refer to the *Creating a Facebook app* and *Creating a test Facebook app and test users* recipes.

We will use a JSP so make sure that the Maven dependency for JSTL is declared in your pom.xml file and the corresponding `ViewResolver` bean is declared in your Spring configuration class. For more details, refer to the *Using a JSP view* recipe in the *Chapter 3, Using Controllers and Views*.

How to do it...

Here are the steps to implement the Facebook OAuth workflow:

1. Add the Maven dependencies for Spring Social and Spring Social Facebook in pom.xml:

```
<dependency>
    <groupId>org.springframework.social</groupId>
    <artifactId>spring-social-core</artifactId>
    <version>1.1.0.RELEASE</version>
</dependency>

<dependency>
    <groupId>org.springframework.social</groupId>
    <artifactId>spring-social-web</artifactId>
    <version>1.1.0.RELEASE</version>
</dependency>

<dependency>
    <groupId>org.springframework.social</groupId>
    <artifactId>spring-social-config</artifactId>
    <version>1.1.0.RELEASE</version>
```

```
    </dependency>

    <dependency>
      <groupId>org.springframework.social</groupId>
      <artifactId>spring-social-facebook</artifactId>
      <version>1.1.1.RELEASE</version>
    </dependency>

    <dependency>
      <groupId>org.springframework.social</groupId>
      <artifactId>spring-social-facebook-web</artifactId>
      <version>1.1.1.RELEASE</version>
    </dependency>
```

2. Create a controller class:

```
@Controller
public class FacebookController {

...
```

3. Create a Facebook login method containing the **App ID** and **App Secret**, which will redirect the user to a Facebook authorization page:

```
@RequestMapping("/fb/login")
public void login(HttpServletResponse response) throws
IOException {
  FacebookConnectionFactory connectionFactory = new
FacebookConnectionFactory("759801647423672",
"1b13515e931b0e2b4b9c620f72761e62");

  OAuth2Parameters params = new OAuth2Parameters();
  params.setRedirectUri
("http://localhost:8080/spring_webapp/fb/callback");
  params.setScope("public_profile");

  OAuth2Operations oauthOperations =
connectionFactory.getOAuthOperations();
  String authorizeUrl =
oauthOperations.buildAuthorizeUrl(params);

  response.sendRedirect(authorizeUrl);
}
```

4. Create the `callback` method for the callback URL, where the user will be redirected after logging in to Facebook. Using the authorization code parameter received from Facebook, get an access token and save it in the session:

```
@RequestMapping("/fb/callback")
public String callback(@RequestParam("code") String
authorizationCode, HttpServletRequest request) {
    FacebookConnectionFactory connectionFactory = new
FacebookConnectionFactory("759801647423672",
"1b13515e931b0e2b4b9c620f72761e62");

    OAuth2Operations oauthOperations =
connectionFactory.getOAuthOperations();
    AccessGrant accessGrant =
oauthOperations.exchangeForAccess(authorizationCode,
"http://localhost:8080/spring_webapp/fb/callback", null);

    String token = accessGrant.getAccessToken();
    request.getSession().setAttribute("facebookToken",
token);

    return "redirect:/fb";
}
```

5. Create a method to display a JSP if the connection to Facebook using the access token in the session is successful. Otherwise, it will redirect the user to the login URL:

```
@RequestMapping("/fb")
public String fb(HttpServletRequest request) {
    String accessToken = (String)
request.getSession().getAttribute("facebookToken");

    Facebook facebook = new FacebookTemplate(accessToken);
    if(facebook.isAuthorized()) {
        return "fb";
    }
    else {
        return "redirect:/fb/login";
    }
}
```

6. Create a JSP for the previous method:

```
<%@ taglib prefix="c"
uri="http://java.sun.com/jsp/jstl/core" %>
<%@ page isELIgnored="false" %>

<html>
```

```
<body>
    <p>Connected to Facebook</p>
</body>
</html>
```

7. To test whether it's working, log out of your Facebook account and go to /fb. You will be redirected to Facebook. Log in, authorize the app, and you will be redirected back to the web application. Remember to use the login credentials of a test user if you are using a test app.

How it works...

The login() method builds a Facebook authorization URL with the **App ID** (https://www.facebook.com/login.php?api_key=759801647423672&redirect_uri=...) and redirects the user to it.

Once the user has authorized the app, he/she is redirected back to our web application to a callback URL, /fb/callback, which we provided in the login() method:

```
params.setRedirectUri
("http://localhost:8080/spring_webapp/fb/callback");
```

The callback URL contains a code parameter provided by Facebook.

In the callback() method, we will use that authorization code to get an OAuth access token that we will store in the session. This is part of the standard OAuth workflow; the access token is not provided directly in the callback URL, so it's never shown to the user. On our server, the **App Secret** (also never shown to the user) is required to obtain the token from the authorization code.

We then redirect the user to /fb. In the fb() method, we retrieve the token from the session and use it to connect to the Facebook user's account.

Retrieving a Facebook user's profile

In this recipe, you'll learn how to retrieve a Facebook user's profile data, which automatically becomes available to the app once the user has authorized it.

Getting ready

This recipe uses the code from the *Connecting to Facebook* recipe.

How to do it...

Here are the steps to retrieve the profile of a Facebook user:

1. In the `FacebookController` class, add a Model argument to the `fb()` method:

   ```
   @RequestMapping("/fb")
   public String fb(HttpServletRequest request, Model model) {
   ...
   ```

2. In the `if(facebook.isAuthorized())` block, use the Facebook object to retrieve the user's profile:

   ```
   FacebookProfile profile =
   facebook.userOperations().getUserProfile();
   ```

3. Pass the user profile to the JSP view:

   ```
   model.addAttribute("profile", profile);
   ```

4. In the JSP, display data from the user's profile:

   ```
   id: ${profile.id}<br />
   username: ${profile.username}<br />
   name: ${profile.name}<br />
   gender: ${profile.gender}<br />
   email: ${profile.email}<br />
   birthday: ${profile.birthday}<br />
   hometown: ${profile.hometown}<br />
   ```

How it works...

Behind the scenes, Spring Social sends a REST HTTP request to `www.facebook.com` and builds a `FacebookProfile` object from the response.

There's more...

For the full list of available fields, look directly in the `FacebookProfile` class.

Some fields of the user profile require additional permissions to be accessible: for example, the e-mail, which requires the `email` permission. Refer to the next recipe where we will extend the scope parameter of the authorization request. The full list of the available permissions can be found at `https://developers.facebook.com/docs/facebook-login/permissions/v2.2`.

Retrieving the list of friends of a Facebook user

In this recipe, you'll learn how to retrieve the friends list of a Facebook user from a Spring web application.

Getting ready

This recipe uses the code from the *Connecting to Facebook* recipe.

How to do it...

Here are the steps to retrieve the list of friends of a Facebook user:

1. In the `FacebookController` class, in the `login()` method, add `user_friends` to the `scope` parameter:

   ```
   params.setScope("public_profile, user_friends");
   ```

2. Add a `Model` argument to the `fb()` method:

   ```
   @RequestMapping("/fb")
   public String fb(HttpServletRequest request, Model model) {
   ...
   ```

3. In the `if(facebook.isAuthorized())` block, use the Facebook object to get the list of friends:

   ```
   List<Reference> friendList =
   facebook.friendOperations().getFriends();
   ```

4. Retrieve the profile of each friend:

   ```
   List<FacebookProfile> friendProfileList = new
   LinkedList<FacebookProfile>();
   for (Reference friend : friendList) {
     FacebookProfile friendProfile =
   facebook.userOperations().getUserProfile(friend.getId());
     friendProfileList.add(friendProfile);
   }
   ```

5. Pass the list of profiles to the JSP view:

   ```
   model.addAttribute("friendProfileList", friendProfileList);
   ```

6. In the JSP, display the profiles of the friends:

```
<c:forEach items="${friendProfileList}" var="profile">
  <h2>${profile.name}</h2>
  <p>
    id: ${profile.id}<br />
    name: ${profile.name}<br />
    gender: ${profile.gender}<br />
  </p>
</c:forEach>
```

How it works...

We retrieved the user's friends using getFriends(). This gave us only their names, so we used getUserProfile() to fetch their public profile.

We added user_friends to the scope parameter, but the user can choose to prevent our Facebook app from accessing his/her friends list. For more information about permissions, go to https://developers.facebook.com/docs/facebook-login/permissions/v2.3.

Posting a Facebook status update

In this recipe, you'll learn how to post a status update on a Facebook user's Timeline from a Spring web application.

Getting ready

This recipe uses the code from the *Connecting to Facebook* recipe.

How to do it...

Here are the steps to post a status update on a Facebook Timeline:

1. In the FacebookController class, in the login() method, add publish_actions to the scope parameter:

    ```
    params.setScope("public_profile, publish_actions");
    ```

2. In the fb() method, in the if(facebook.isAuthorized()) block, use the Facebook object to post the status update:

    ```
    facebook.feedOperations().updateStatus("This was posted from a Spring web application.");
    ```

Posting a link to Facebook

In this recipe, you'll learn how to post a link on a Facebook user's Timeline from a Spring web application.

Getting ready

This recipe uses the code from the *Connecting to Facebook* recipe.

How to do it...

Here are the steps to post a link on a Facebook user's Timeline:

1. In the `FacebookController` class, in the `login()` method, add `publish_actions` to the `scope` parameter:

    ```
    params.setScope("public_profile, publish_actions");
    ```

2. In the `fb()` method, in the `if(facebook.isAuthorized())` block, create a `FacebookLink` object with the link URL, title, caption, and description:

    ```
    FacebookLink link = new
    FacebookLink("http://jeromejaglale.com/",
        "Spring is easy with Spring Cookbook",
        "Spring Cookbook",
        "The recipes are understandable and actually work.");
    ```

3. Use the Facebook object to post the link:

    ```
    facebook.feedOperations().postLink("This link was posted
    from a Spring web application.", link);
    ```

4. In your browser, go to `/fb`. Then, go to the user's Facebook account and verify that the link has been posted.

Posting a custom object to Facebook

In this recipe, you'll learn how to post a custom object to a Facebook user's Timeline from a Spring web application. A custom object is a link with more customizable options: picture, privacy, and location. In this recipe, we will add a picture to a link.

Getting ready

This recipe uses the code from the *Connecting to Facebook* recipe.

How to do it...

Here are the steps to post a custom object:

1. In the `FacebookController` class, in the `login()` method, add `publish_actions` to the `scope` parameter:

   ```
   params.setScope("public_profile, publish_actions");
   ```

2. In the `fb()` method, in the `if(facebook.isAuthorized())` block, create a `PostData` object using the Facebook object:

   ```
   PostData postData = new
   PostData(facebook.userOperations().getUserProfile().getId());
   ```

3. Initialize the different fields of the custom object:

```
postData.message("Vegetables are good for you.");
postData.link("http://jeromejaglale.com");
postData.caption("Pasta and vegetables");
postData.description("Carbs are fine. Just don't forget
your vegetables.");
postData.picture("http://jeromejaglale.com/images/
photo/vancouver_summer_2007/aa_02_appetissant.JPG");
```

4. Use the Facebook object to post the custom object:

```
facebook.feedOperations().post(postData);
```

5. In your browser, go to /fb. Then, go to the user's Facebook account and verify that the custom object has been posted.

Creating a Twitter application

A web application can access a Twitter account only through a Twitter application. In this recipe, we will create a Twitter application. We will obtain an **API key** and an **API secret**, which are two strings that our web application will use to connect to Twitter in the following recipes.

Getting ready

Log in to your Twitter account.

How to do it...

1. Go to `https://apps.twitter.com/`.
2. Click on **Create New App**.
3. Fill in the form and create your application. Note that `localhost` is not a valid domain name for the **Callback URL** field, but an IP address works.
4. On your application page, under **Settings**, check **Allow this application to be used to Sign in with Twitter**.
5. Under **Keys and Access Tokens**, copy the **API key** and **API secret** values. You will use them in your web application to identify your Twitter application.

Connecting to Twitter

Twitter allows access to a user account through an OAuth workflow; from our web application, the user is redirected to a Twitter page to authorize the Twitter application in order to access his/her account. The user is then redirected back to our web application. In this recipe, we'll implement this OAuth workflow.

Getting ready

You need an existing Twitter application. Refer to the *Creating a Twitter application recipe*.

We will use a JSP, so make sure that the Maven dependency for JSTL is declared in your `pom.xml` file and the corresponding `ViewResolver` bean is declared in your Spring configuration class. For more details, refer to the *Using a JSP view* recipe in *Chapter 3, Using Controllers and Views*.

How to do it...

Here are the steps to implement the Twitter OAuth workflow:

1. Add the Maven dependencies for Spring Social and Spring Social Twitter in `pom.xml`:

```
<dependency>
    <groupId>org.springframework.social</groupId>
    <artifactId>spring-social-core</artifactId>
    <version>1.1.0.RELEASE</version>
</dependency>

<dependency>
    <groupId>org.springframework.social</groupId>
    <artifactId>spring-social-web</artifactId>
    <version>1.1.0.RELEASE</version>
</dependency>

<dependency>
    <groupId>org.springframework.social</groupId>
    <artifactId>spring-social-config</artifactId>
    <version>1.1.0.RELEASE</version>
</dependency>

<dependency>
  <groupId>org.springframework.social</groupId>
  <artifactId>spring-social-twitter</artifactId>
  <version>1.1.0.RELEASE</version>
</dependency>
```

2. Create a controller class:

```
@Controller
public class TwitterController {
...
```

3. Create a Twitter login method containing your API key and API secret, which will redirect to Twitter's authorization page:

```
@RequestMapping("/tw/login")
public void login(HttpServletRequest request,
HttpServletResponse response) throws IOException {
  TwitterConnectionFactory connectionFactory = new
TwitterConnectionFactory("YtAG8npnZkUFDghkF2V3ykm0P",
"RQ6hGGALfEaWGh6Vu03xcFtM1ibicW8IwSUBKaLG4drvVXXaay");
```

```
    OAuth1Operations oauthOperations =
connectionFactory.getOAuthOperations();

    OAuthToken requestToken =
oauthOperations.fetchRequestToken("http://
jeromejaglale.com:8080/spring_webapp/tw/callback", null);
    request.getSession().setAttribute("requestToken",
requestToken);
    String authorizeUrl =
oauthOperations.buildAuthenticateUrl(requestToken.getValue(
), OAuth1Parameters.NONE);

    response.sendRedirect(authorizeUrl);
}
```

4. Create the `callback` method, where the user will be redirected after logging in to Twitter. Use the `oauth_verifier` parameter received from Twitter as well as the request token from `login()` to get an access token and save it in the session:

```
@RequestMapping("/tw/callback")
public String callback(String oauth_token, String
oauth_verifier, HttpServletRequest request) {
   TwitterConnectionFactory connectionFactory = new
TwitterConnectionFactory("YtAG8npnZkUFDghkF2V3ykm0P",
"RQ6hGGALfEaWGh6Vu03xcFtM1ibicW8IwSUBKaLG4drvVXXaay");

   OAuthToken requestToken = (OAuthToken)
request.getSession().getAttribute("requestToken");
   OAuth1Operations oAuthOperations =
connectionFactory.getOAuthOperations();
   OAuthToken token =
oAuthOperations.exchangeForAccessToken(new
AuthorizedRequestToken(requestToken, oauth_verifier),
null);

   request.getSession().setAttribute("twitterToken", token);

   return "redirect:/tw";
}
```

5. Create a method that will display a JSP if it manages to connect to Twitter. Otherwise, it will redirect to the login URL:

```
@RequestMapping("/tw")
public String tw(HttpServletRequest request) {
   OAuthToken token = (OAuthToken)
request.getSession().getAttribute("twitterToken");
```

```
    if(token == null) {
      return "redirect:/tw/login";
    }

    TwitterConnectionFactory connectionFactory = new
TwitterConnectionFactory("YtAG8npnZkUFDghkF2V3ykm0P",
"RQ6hGGALfEaWGh6Vu03xcFtM1ibicW8IwSUBKaLG4drvVXXaay");
    Connection<Twitter> connection =
connectionFactory.createConnection(token);
    Twitter twitter = connection.getApi();
    if( ! twitter.isAuthorized()) {
      return "redirect:/tw/login";
    }

    return "tw";
}
```

6. Create a JSP for the previous method:

```
<%@ taglib prefix="c"
uri="http://java.sun.com/jsp/jstl/core" %>
<%@ page isELIgnored="false" %>
<html>
<body>
    <p>Connected to Twitter</p>
</body>
</html>
```

How it works...

The `login()` method builds a Twitter authorization URL using the API key and redirects the user to it.

Authorize spring_cookbook to use your account?

spring_cookbook

jeromejaglale.com

Just for testing

Username or email

Password

☐ Remember me · Forgot password?

Sign In **Cancel**

This application will be able to:

- Read Tweets from your timeline.
- See who you follow, and follow new people.
- Update your profile.
- Post Tweets for you.

Will not be able to:

- Access your direct messages.
- See your Twitter password.

Once the user has authorized our Twitter application, he/she is redirected back to our web application to a *callback URL*, `/tw/callback`, that we provided with this line:

```
OAuthToken requestToken =
oauthOperations.fetchRequestToken("http://jeromejaglale.com:8080/
spring_webapp/tw/callback", null);
```

The callback URL contains a `oauth_verifier` parameter provided by Twitter.

In the `callback()` method, we use this authorization code to get an OAuth access token that we store in the session. This is part of the standard OAuth workflow; the token is not provided directly, so it's not shown to the user. On our server, the application secret (also never shown to the user) is required to obtain the token from the authorization code.

We then redirect the user to `/tw`. In the `tw()` method, we retrieve the token from the session and use it to connect to the user's Twitter account.

Retrieving a user's Twitter profile

In this recipe, you'll learn how to retrieve a user's Twitter profile data, which automatically becomes available to the Twitter application once the user has authorized the Twitter application.

Getting ready

This recipe uses the code from the *Connecting to Twitter* recipe.

How to do it...

Here are the steps to retrieve data from the profile of a Twitter user:

1. In the `TwitterController` class, add a `Model` argument to the `tw()` method:

   ```
   @RequestMapping("/fw")
   public String fb(HttpServletRequest request, Model model) {
   ...
   ```

2. In that method, use the Twitter object to retrieve the user profile:

   ```
   TwitterProfile profile =
   twitter.userOperations().getUserProfile();
   ```

3. Pass the user profile to the JSP view:

   ```
   model.addAttribute("profile", profile);
   ```

4. In the JSP, display data from the user profile:

   ```
   name: ${profile.name}<br />
   screenName: ${profile.screenName}<br />
   url: ${profile.url}<br />
   profileImageUrl: ${profile.profileImageUrl}<br />
   description: ${profile.description}<br />
   location: ${profile.location}<br />
   createdDate: ${profile.createdDate}<br />
   language: ${profile.language}<br />
   statusesCount: ${profile.statusesCount}<br />
   followersCount: ${profile.followersCount}<br />
   ```

Retrieving the tweets of a Twitter user

In this recipe, you'll learn how to retrieve the last tweets of a Twitter user from a Spring web application.

Getting ready

This recipe uses the code from the *Connecting to Twitter* recipe.

How to do it...

Here are the steps to retrieve the last tweets of a Twitter user:

1. In the `TwitterController` class, add a `Model` argument to the `tw()` method:

   ```
   @RequestMapping("/fw")
   public String fb(HttpServletRequest request, Model model) {
   ...
   ```

2. In that method, use the Twitter object to retrieve the user's tweets:

   ```
   List<Tweet> tweets =
   twitter.timelineOperations().getUserTimeline();
   ```

3. Pass the list of tweets to the JSP view:

   ```
   model.addAttribute("tweets", tweets);
   ```

4. In the JSP, display the list of tweets:

   ```
   <c:forEach items="${tweets}" var="tweet">
     <p>${tweet.text}</p>
   </c:forEach>
   ```

Posting a tweet to Twitter

In this recipe, you'll learn how to post a tweet on behalf of a user from a Spring web application.

Getting ready

This recipe uses the code from the *Connecting to Twitter* recipe.

How to do it...

In the `TwitterController` class, in the `tw()` method, use the Twitter object to post a tweet.

```
twitter.timelineOperations().updateStatus("Just a test");
```

Sending a private message to another Twitter user

In this recipe, you'll learn how to send a private message to another Twitter user from a Spring web application. Note that the user who is the recipient has to be a follower of the user who is the sender.

Getting Ready

This recipe uses the code from the *Connecting to Twitter* recipe.

How to do it...

In the **TwitterController** class, in the **tw()** method, use the Twitter object to send a private message to another Twitter user:

```
twitter.directMessageOperations().sendDirectMessage(
"jeromejaglale", "Hey Jerome, I'm just testing your recipe.");
```

11
Using the Java RMI, HTTP Invoker, Hessian, and REST

In this chapter, we will cover the following recipes:

- ▸ Creating a Java RMI service
- ▸ Querying an existing Java RMI service
- ▸ Creating an HTTP Invoker service
- ▸ Querying an existing HTTP Invoker service
- ▸ Creating a Hessian service
- ▸ Querying an existing Hessian service
- ▸ Creating a REST service
- ▸ Querying an existing REST service

Introduction

This chapter is about making Spring interact with another piece of software over a network. Different protocols can be used for this, but each one of them uses a client/server architecture. Spring can be the client or server.

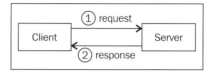

Java RMI and HTTP Invoker are remote method invocation technologies; a Java client executes a method located on a Java server just as with a normal method. The request contains the method's arguments and the response contains the method's return value.

Hessian, REST, and SOAP are web services; the request is an HTTP request to a web server, which sends back an HTTP response. Web services are platform agnostic; for example, the client could be a Spring application (Java) and the server could be a PHP application.

REST is currently the most popular option; it's simple, flexible, and cross-platform.

As a rule of thumb, use:

▶ HTTP Invoker to interact with another Spring application

▶ Java RMI to interact with another Java application not using Spring

▶ Hessian to interact with another Java application not using Spring when you need to go over proxies and firewalls

▶ SOAP if you have to; it won't be covered in this chapter

▶ REST for all other cases

Creating a Java RMI service

The Java RMI is a Java remote method invocation technology; a client executes a method ocated on a server, the Java RMI service.

In this recipe, we will set up a Java RMI service that will expose the methods of a normal Java class. The service will be part of an existing Spring web application but will use its own port.

Getting ready

The server will expose the methods of the `UserService` interface:

```
Public interface UserService {
  public abstract List<User> findAll();
  public abstract void addUser(User user);
}
```

The `UserService` interface is implemented by `UserServiceImpl`:

```
public class UserServiceImpl implements UserService {
  private List<User> userList = new LinkedList<User>();

  public UserServiceImpl() {
    User user1 = new User("Merlin", 777);
    userList.add(user1);

    User user2 = new User("Arthur", 123);
    userList.add(user2);
  }

  public List<User> findAll() {
    return userList;
  }

  public void addUser(User user) {
    userList.add(user);
  }
}
```

The `UserService` methods will receive and send `User` objects:

```
public class User implements Serializable {
  private String name;
  private int age;

  public User(String name, int age) {
    this.name = name;
    this.age = age;
  }

  // ... getters and setters
}
```

Note that the `User` class implements `Serializable`; this is necessary because the `User` objects are serialized before they are transmitted over the network.

How to do it...

Here are the steps to create a Java RMI service:

1. In the Spring configuration, add a `UserService` bean returning an instance of `UserServiceImpl`:

```
@Bean
public UserService userService() {
  return new UserServiceImpl();
}
```

2. Add an `RmiServiceExporter` bean. Define the Java RMI service name, the interface exposed by the service, and the object implementing it:

```
@Bean
public RmiServiceExporter rmiServiceExporter() {
  RmiServiceExporter rmiServiceExporter = new
RmiServiceExporter();
    rmiServiceExporter.setServiceName("userService");
    rmiServiceExporter.setServiceInterface(UserService.class);
    rmiServiceExporter.setService(userService());
    return rmiServiceExporter;
}
```

3. The Java RMI service is now available at `rmi://localhost:1099/userService`.

How it works...

`RmiServiceExporter` is a Spring class generating an RMI service from a Java interface (`UserService`). For each method defined in `UserService`, the corresponding method from `userService()`, in `UserServiceImpl`, will be executed. The RMI service is made available by default on the `1099` port.

Querying an existing Java RMI service

In this recipe, we will configure a Spring web application, so that it will be able to execute a method on an existing RMI service.

Getting ready

We will query the Java RMI service of the previous *Creating a Java RMI service* recipe.

We need the `UserService` interface so that our application knows the methods available on the RMI service:

```
public interface UserService {
  public abstract List
  public abstract void addUser(User user);
}
```

`User` objects will be exchanged over the network, so we need the `User` class of the previous recipe as well:

```
public class User implements Serializable {
  private String name;
  private int age;

  public User(String name, int age) {
    this.name = name;
    this.age = age;
  }

  // ... getters and setters
}
```

In real applications, these classes could be provided to the RMI client as a JAR file.

How to do it...

Here are the steps to query a Java RMI service:

1. In the Spring configuration, add a `RmiProxyFactoryBean` bean named `userService`. Define the Java RMI service URL and the `UserService` interface:

    ```
    @Bean(name="userService")
    public RmiProxyFactoryBean rmiProxyFactoryBean() {
      RmiProxyFactoryBean rmiProxyFactoryBean = new
    RmiProxyFactoryBean();
      rmiProxyFactoryBean.setServiceUrl("rmi://localhost:1099/
    userService");
      rmiProxyFactoryBean.setServiceInterface(UserService.class);
      return rmiProxyFactoryBean;
    }
    ```

2. In a controller class, add an autowired `UserService` field:

```
@Controller
public class UserController {
  @Autowired
  private UserService userService;
```

3. In a controller method, execute the `findAll()` method of the `UserService` object:

```
@RequestMapping("user_list")
@ResponseBody
public void userList() {
  List<User> userList = userService.findAll();
}
```

How it works...

The autowired `UserService` object is created behind the scenes by Spring. It's actually an `RmiProxyFactoryBean` object that will delegate the execution of the `findAll()` method to the Java RMI service located at `rmi://localhost:1099/userService`.

Creating an HTTP Invoker service

HTTP Invoker, like the Java RMI, is a Java remote method invocation technology; here, a client executes a method located on a server-the HTTP invoker service. HTTP is used instead of a custom port, so it can go over proxies and firewalls. However, it's a Spring technology, so both the client and the server must use Java and Spring.

In this recipe, we will set up an HTTP Invoker service that will expose the methods of a normal Java class. The service will be part of an existing Spring web application.

Getting ready

The server will expose the methods of the `UserService` interface:

```
public interface UserService {
  public abstract List<User> findAll();
  public abstract void addUser(User user);
}
```

The `UserService` interface is implemented by `UserServiceImpl`:

```
public class UserServiceImpl implements UserService {
  private List<User> userList = new LinkedList<User>();

  public UserServiceImpl() {
```

```
    User user1 = new User("Merlin", 777);
    userList.add(user1);

    User user2 = new User("Arthur", 123);
    userList.add(user2);
  }

  public List<User> findAll() {
    return userList;
  }

  public void addUser(User user) {
    userList.add(user);
  }
}
```

The `UserService` methods will receive and send `User` objects:

```
public class User implements Serializable {
  private String name;
  private int age;

  public User(String name, int age) {
    this.name = name;
    this.age = age;
  }

  // ... getters and setters
}
```

 Note that the `User` class implements `Serializable`; it's necessary because `User` objects are serialized before they are transmitted over the network.

How to do it...

Here are the steps to create an HTTP Invoker service:

1. In the Spring configuration, add a `UserService` bean returning an instance of `UserServiceImpl`:

    ```
    @Bean
    public UserService userService() {
      return new UserServiceImpl();
    }
    ```

2. Add an `HttpInvokerServiceExporter` bean named `/userService`. Define the interface exposed by the service and the object implementing it:

```
@Bean(name = "/userService")
public HttpInvokerServiceExporter
httpInvokerServiceExporter() {
  HttpInvokerServiceExporter exporter = new
HttpInvokerServiceExporter();
  exporter.setService(userService());
  exporter.setServiceInterface(UserService.class);
  return exporter;
}
```

3. The HTTP Invoker service is now available at the `/userService` URL of the Spring web application.

How it works...

`HttpInvokerServiceExporter` is a Spring class generating an HTTP Invoker service from a Java interface (`UserService`). For each method defined in `UserService`, the corresponding method from `userService()`, in `UserServiceImpl`, will be executed.

Querying an existing HTTP Invoker service

In this recipe, we will configure a Spring web application that will be able to execute a method on an existing HTTP Invoker service.

Getting ready

We will query the HTTP Invoker service of the previous *Creating an HTTP Invoker service* recipe.

We need the `UserService` interface so that our application knows the methods available on the HTTP Invoker service:

```
public interface UserService {
  public abstract List<User> findAll();
  public abstract void addUser(User user);
}
```

`User` objects will be exchanged over the network, so we need the `User` class of the previous recipe as well:

```
public class User implements Serializable {
  private String name;
```

```
   private int age;

   public User(String name, int age) {
     this.name = name;
     this.age = age;
   }

   // ... getters and setters
}
```

How to do it...

Here are the steps for using an HTTP Invoker service:

1. In the Spring configuration, add an `HttpInvokerProxyFactoryBean` bean named `userService`. Define the HTTP Invoker service URL and the `UserService` interface:

    ```
    @Bean(name="userService")
    public HttpInvokerProxyFactoryBean userService() {
      HttpInvokerProxyFactoryBean factory = new
    HttpInvokerProxyFactoryBean();

    factory.setServiceUrl("http://localhost:8080/
    http_invoker_server/userService");
        factory.setServiceInterface(UserService.class);
        return factory;
    }
    ```

2. In a controller class, add a `UserService` field as a standard autowired service bean:

    ```
    @Controller
    public class UserController {
      @Autowired
      private UserService userService;
    ```

3. In a controller method, execute the `findAll()` method of the `UserService` object and log the results:

    ```
    @RequestMapping("user_list")
    @ResponseBody
    public void userList() {
      List<User> userList = userService.findAll();
      for (User user : userList) {
    ```

```
        System.out.println("User " + user.getAge() + " is " +
    user.getAge() + " years old");
      }
    }
```

How it works...

In the `UserController` class, the autowired `UserService` object is instantiated behind the scenes by Spring. It's actually an `HttpInvokerProxyFactoryBean`, which will delegate the execution of the `findAll()` method to the HTTP Invoker service located at `http://localhost:8080/http_invoker_server/userService`.

Creating a Hessian service

Hessian is a remote method invocation technology; here, a client executes a method located on a server-the Hessian service. It uses HTTP, so it can go over proxies and firewalls. It also has implementations in multiple languages (PHP, Python, Ruby, and so on). So, for example, the client can use Java and the server can use PHP.

In this recipe, we will add a Hessian service to an existing Spring web application. It will expose the methods of a Java class.

Getting ready

The server will expose the methods of the `UserService` interface:

```
public interface UserService {
  public abstract List<User> findAll();
  public abstract void addUser(User user);
}
```

The `UserService` interface is implemented by `UserServiceImpl`:

```
public class UserServiceImpl implements UserService {
  private List<User> userList = new LinkedList<User>();

  public UserServiceImpl() {
    User user1 = new User("Merlin", 777);
    userList.add(user1);

    User user2 = new User("Arthur", 123);
    userList.add(user2);
  }
```

```
    public List<User> findAll() {
      return userList;
    }

    public void addUser(User user) {
      userList.add(user);
    }
}
```

The `UserService` methods will receive and send `User` objects:

```
public class User {
    private String name;
    private int age;

    public User(String name, int age) {
      this.name = name;
      this.age = age;
    }

    // ... getters and setters
}
```

 Note that the `User` class doesn't need to implement `Serializable`. Hessian uses its own object serialization mechanism.

How to do it...

Here are the steps to create a Hessian service:

1. In the Spring configuration, add a `UserService` bean returning an instance of `UserServiceImpl`:

    ```
    @Bean
    public UserService userService() {
      return new UserServiceImpl();
    }
    ```

2. Add a `HessianServiceExporter` bean named `/userService`. Define the interface exposed by the service and the object implementing it:

    ```
    @Bean(name = "/userService")
    public HessianServiceExporter hessianServiceExporter () {
      HessianServiceExporterexporter = new
    HessianServiceExporter ();
      exporter.setService(userService());
    ```

```
      exporter.setServiceInterface(UserService.class);
      return exporter;
   }
```

3. The Hessian service is now available at the `/userService` URL of the Spring web application.

How it works...

`HessianServiceExporter` is a Spring class generating a Hessian service from a Java interface (`UserService`). For each method defined in `UserService`, the corresponding method from `userService()`, in `UserServiceImpl`, will be executed.

Querying an existing Hessian service

In this recipe, we will configure a Spring web application, so that it will be able to execute a method on an existing Hessian service.

Getting ready

We will query the Hessian service of the previous *Creating a Hessian service* recipe.

We need the `UserService` interface, so that our application knows the methods available on the Hessian service:

```
public interface UserService {
  public abstract List<User> findAll();
  public abstract void addUser(User user);
}
```

`User` objects will be exchanged over the network, so we need the `User` class of the previous recipe as well:

```
public class User implements Serializable {
  private String name;
  private int age;

  public User(String name, int age) {
    this.name = name;
    this.age = age;
  }

  // ... getters and setters
}
```

How to do it...

Here are the steps for using a Hessian service:

1. In the Spring configuration, add a `HessianProxyFactoryBean` bean named `userService`. Define the Hessian service URL and the `UserService` interface:

```
@Bean(name="userService")
public HessianProxyFactoryBean userService() {
   HessianProxyFactoryBean factory = new
HessianProxyFactoryBean();

   factory.setServiceUrl("http://localhost:8080/
hessian_server/userService");
      factory.setServiceInterface(UserService.class);
      return factory;
}
```

2. In a controller class, add a `UserService` field as a standard autowired service bean:

```
@Controller
public class UserController {
   @Autowired
   private UserService userService;
```

3. In a controller method, execute the `findAll()` method of the `UserService` object and log the results:

```
@RequestMapping("user_list")
@ResponseBody
public void userList() {
   List<User> userList = userService.findAll();
   for (User user : userList) {
      System.out.println("User " + user.getAge() + " is " +
user.getAge() + " years old");
   }
}
```

How it works...

In the `UserController` class, the autowired `UserService` object is instantiated behind the scenes by Spring. It's actually a `HessianProxyFactoryBean` that will delegate the execution of the `findAll()` method to the Hessian service located at `http://localhost:8080/hessian/userService`.

Creating a REST service

REST uses a web service architecture; here, a client sends an HTTP request to a server, which sends back an HTTP response. JSON is most of the time used for data transfer. The list of URLs supported by the server is called the REST API. These URLs are kept simple using different HTTP methods. For example, the `/users/3` request using the GET method will return the user whose ID is 3. The `/users/3` request using the DELETE method will delete that same user.

In this recipe, we will create a simple REST service that will allow a REST client to query and modify a list of `User` objects on the server.

Getting ready

We will use the `User` class:

```java
public class User {

  private Long id;
  private String name;
  private int age;

  public User() {
  }

  public User(Long id, String name, int age) {
    this.id = id;
    this.name = name;
    this.age = age;
  }

  // ... getters and setters
}
```

We will use the `UserService` class with a preset list of users:

```java
public class UserService {

  List<User> userList = new LinkedList<User>();

  public UserService() {
    User user1 = new User(1L, "Merlin", 777);
```

```
      userList.add(user1);

      User user2 = new User(2L, "Arthur", 123);
      userList.add(user2);
    }

    public List<User> findAll() {
      return userList;
    }

    public User findUser(Long id) {
      for (User user : userList) {
        if(user.getId().equals(id)) {
          return user;
        }
      }
      return null;
    }
  }
```

How to do it...

Here are the steps to create a REST service:

1. Add the Maven dependencies for `jackson` in `pom.xml`:

   ```
   <dependency>
     <groupId>com.fasterxml.jackson.core</groupId>
     <artifactId>jackson-core</artifactId>
     <version>2.4.2</version>
   </dependency>

   <dependency>
     <groupId>com.fasterxml.jackson.core</groupId>
     <artifactId>jackson-databind</artifactId>
     <version>2.4.2</version>
   </dependency>
   ```

2. In the Spring configuration, add a `UserService` bean:

   ```
   @Bean
   public UserService userService() {
     return new UserService();
   }
   ```

3. Create a controller class with a URL prefix annotated with `@RestController`:

```
@RestController
@RequestMapping("users*")
public class UserController {
}
```

4. Add an autowired `UserService` field:

```
@Autowired
private UserService userService;
```

5. Add a controller method returning the list of all users:

```
@RequestMapping
public List<User> userList() {
  List<User> userList = userService.findAll();
  return userList;
}
```

6. Add a controller method returning the user corresponding to a given ID:

```
@RequestMapping("/{id}")
public User findUser(@PathVariable("id") Long userId) {
  User user = userService.findUser(userId);
  return user;
}
```

7. The Spring web application is now a REST service. It will return User objects serialized to JSON in response to the `/users` and `/users/1` URL requests.

How it works...

`UserController` is a standard Spring controller except for the `@RestController` annotation, which will automatically convert the objects returned by the controller methods to JSON, using the Jackson library.

There's more...

To use a specific HTTP method, add the `method` argument in the `@RequestMapping` annotation:

```
@RequestMapping(value = "/{id}", method = RequestMethod.POST)
```

To secure a REST service:

- ▸ Use HTTPS so that data transfers between the client and server are encrypted. Refer to the *Using HTTPS with Tomcat* recipe in *Chapter 6, Managing Security*.

- ▸ If you want only authorized clients to query it, you can use HTTP Basic Authentication. Refer to the *Authenticating users using the default login page* recipe from *Chapter 6, Managing Security*, especially, the `httpBasic()` method. Another possibility is to use an OAuth workflow. It's more complicated, but it avoids the client having to send a username and password at each request. That's the method chosen by Facebook and Twitter for their REST API, for example.

Querying an existing REST service

In this recipe, from a Spring controller method, we will retrieve data from an existing REST service.

Getting ready

We will query the REST service of the previous *Creating a REST service* recipe.

We will convert the JSON data received from the REST service to `User` objects. We will use this `User` class:

```
public class User implements {
  private String name;
  private int age;

  // ... getters and setters
}
```

How to do it...

Here are the steps for using a REST service:

1. Add the Maven dependencies for Jackson in `pom.xml`:

```
<dependency>
  <groupId>com.fasterxml.jackson.core</groupId>
  <artifactId>jackson-core</artifactId>
  <version>2.4.2</version>
</dependency>

<dependency>
  <groupId>com.fasterxml.jackson.core</groupId>
```

```
        <artifactId>jackson-databind</artifactId>
        <version>2.4.2</version>
    </dependency>
```

2. In a controller method, define the URL of the REST service to query:

```
String url = "http://localhost:8080/rest_server/users/2";
```

3. Use the `RestTemplate` class and its `getForObject()` method to query the REST service and generate a `User` object from the JSON response:

```
RestTemplate restTemplate = new RestTemplate();
User user = restTemplate.getForObject(url, User.class);
```

How it works...

`RestTemplate` is a class provided by Spring that provides methods to easily query REST services and generate Java objects from the received JSON response.

There's more...

If the response is a list of objects, pass an array class as a second parameter to generate an array of objects:

```
User[] userList = restTemplate.getForObject(url, User[].class);
```

12
Using Aspect-oriented Programming

In this chapter, we will cover the following recipes:

- ▶ Creating a Spring AOP aspect class
- ▶ Measuring the execution time of methods using an around advice
- ▶ Logging method arguments using a before advice
- ▶ Logging methods' return values using an after-returning advice
- ▶ Logging exceptions using an after-throwing advice
- ▶ Using an after advice to clean up resources
- ▶ Making a class implement an interface at runtime using an introduction
- ▶ Setting the execution order of the aspects

Introduction

Aspect-oriented programming (**AOP**) is about inserting and executing, at runtime, extra pieces of code at various points of the normal execution flow of a program. In AOP terminology, these pieces of code are methods that are called **advices** and the classes containing them are called **aspects**. AOP is complementary to object-oriented programming.

This chapter is about the Spring AOP framework, which enables us to execute advices before and after methods of Spring beans (controller methods, service methods, and so on). For more extensive AOP functionality, **AspectJ** is the reference Java AOP framework and gets integrated seamlessly with Spring. However, it's more complex to use and requires a customized compilation process.

In the first recipe, we will create an aspect class and configure Spring to use it. We will use this aspect class in the following recipes, where we will go through the different types of advice offered by Spring AOP, using practical use cases.

Creating a Spring AOP aspect class

In this recipe, we will create an aspect class and configure Spring to use it. We will use this aspect class and its configuration code in the following recipes.

How to do it...

Here are the steps for creating an aspect class:

1. Add the the AspectJ Weaver Maven dependency in `pom.xml`:

```
<dependency>
  <groupId>org.aspectj</groupId>
  <artifactId>aspectjweaver</artifactId>
  <version>1.8.5</version>
</dependency>
```

2. Create a Java package for the aspects of your application. For example, `com.springcookbook.aspect`.

3. In your aspects package, create a class annotated with `@Component` and `@Aspect`:

```
@Component
@Aspect
public class Aspect1 {


}
```

4. In the Spring configuration, add `@EnableAspectJAutoProxy` and your aspects package to `@ComponentScan`:

```
@Configuration
@EnableAspectJAutoProxy
@ComponentScan(basePackages =
{"com.spring_cookbook.controllers",
"com.spring_cookbook.aspect"})
public class AppConfig {
...
}
```

How it works...

The AspectJ Weaver Maven dependency provides aspect annotations, so we can use regular Java classes to define aspects.

In the aspect class, `@Aspect` declares the class as an aspect. `@Component` allows it to be detected by Spring and instantiated as a bean.

In the Spring configuration, we included our aspect package in `@ComponentScan`, so the `@Component` classes in that package will be detected and instantiated as beans by Spring. `@EnableAspectJAutoProxy` in the Spring configuration will make Spring actually use the aspects and execute their advices.

Measuring the execution time of methods using an around advice

An **around advice** is the most powerful type of advice; it can completely replace the target method by some different code. In this recipe, we will use it only to execute some extra code before and after the target method. With the before code, we will get the current time. With the after code, we will get the current time again, and will compare it to the previous time to calculate the total time the target method took to execute. Our target methods will be the controller methods of the controller classes in the controller package.

Getting ready

We will use the aspect class defined in the previous recipe, *Creating a Spring AOP aspect class*.

How to do it...

Here are the steps for measuring the execution time of controller methods:

1. In the aspect class, create an advice method annotated with `@Around` and take `ProceedingJoinPoint` as an argument:

```
@Around("execution(*
com.spring_cookbook.controllers.*.*(..))")
public Object doBasicProfiling(ProceedingJoinPoint
joinPoint) throws Throwable {
...
}
```

2. In that advice method, measure the execution time of the target method:

```
Long t1 = System.currentTimeMillis();
Object returnValue = joinPoint.proceed();
Long t2 = System.currentTimeMillis();
Long executionTime = t2 - t1;
```

3. Log that execution time preceded by the target method name:

```
String className =
joinPoint.getSignature().getDeclaringTypeName();
String methodName = joinPoint.getSignature().getName();
System.out.println(className + "." + methodName + "() took
" + executionTime + " ms");
```

4. Return the return value of the target method:

```
return returnValue;
```

5. To test the advice, you can use a controller method that takes a long time on purpose:

```
@RequestMapping("user_list")
@ResponseBody
public void userList() throws Exception {
  try {
      Thread.sleep(2500);   // wait 2.5 seconds
  } catch(InterruptedException ex) {
      Thread.currentThread().interrupt();
  }
}
```

6. Test whether it's working. When going to /user_list in your browser, you should see this in your server log:

```
com.spring_cookbook.controllers.UserController.userList()
took 2563 ms
```

How it works...

The @Around annotation preceding the advice method is a pointcut expression:

```
@Around("execution(* com.spring_cookbook.controllers.*.*(..))")
```

A pointcut expression determines the target methods (the methods to which the advice will be applied). It works like a regular expression. Here, it matches all controller methods. In detail:

- `execution()` means we are targeting a method execution
- The first asterisk means *any return type*
- The second asterisk means *any class* (from the `com.spring_cookbook.controllers` package)
- The third asterisk means *any method*
- `(..)` means *any number of method arguments of any type*

The `joinPoint.proceed()` instruction executes the target method. Skipping this will skip the execution of the target method. A **join point** is another AOP term. It's a moment in the execution flow of the program where an advice can be executed. With Spring AOP, a join point always designates a target method. To summarize, an advice method is applied at different join points, which are identified by a pointcut expression.

We also use the `joinPoint` object to get the name of the current target method:

```
String className =
joinPoint.getSignature().getDeclaringTypeName();
String methodName = joinPoint.getSignature().getName();
```

Logging method arguments using a before advice

A **before advice** executes some extra code before the execution of the target method. In this recipe, we will log the arguments of the target method.

Getting ready

We will use the aspect class defined in the *Creating a Spring AOP aspect class* recipe.

How to do it...

Here are the steps for logging the methods' arguments using a before advice:

1. In your aspect class, create an advice method annotated with `@Before` and take `JoinPoint` as an argument:

```
@Before("execution(*
com.spring_cookbook.controllers.*.*(..))")
public void logArguments(JoinPoint joinPoint) {
...
}
```

2. In that method, get the list of arguments of the target method:

```
Object[] arguments = joinPoint.getArgs();
```

3. Log the list of arguments preceded by the target method name:

```
String className =
joinPoint.getSignature().getDeclaringTypeName();
String methodName = joinPoint.getSignature().getName();
System.out.println("-----" + className + "." + methodName +
"() -----");

for (int i = 0; i < arguments.length; i++) {
  System.out.println(arguments[i]);
}
```

4. Test the advice using a controller method with arguments:

```
@RequestMapping("user_list")
@ResponseBody
public String userList(Locale locale, WebRequest request) {
...
}
```

5. Check whether it's working. When going to /user_list in your browser, you should see this in your server log:

```
-----
com.spring_cookbook.controllers.UserController.userList()
-----
en_US
ServletWebRequest:
uri=/spring_webapp/user_list;client=10.0.2.2
```

How it works...

The @Before annotation preceding the advice method is a pointcut expression:

```
@Before("execution(* com.spring_cookbook.controllers.*.*(..))")
```

Refer to the *Measuring the execution time of methods using an around advice* recipe for more details.

The joinPoint.getArgs() instruction retrieves the argument's values of the target method.

Logging methods' return values using an after-returning advice

An **after-returning advice** executes some extra code after the successful execution of the target method. In this recipe, we will log the return value of the target method.

Getting ready

We will use the aspect class defined in the *Creating a Spring AOP aspect class* recipe.

How to do it...

Here are the steps for logging the return value of methods using an after-returning advice:

1. In your aspect class, create an advice method annotated with `@AfterReturning`. Make it take a `JoinPoint` object and the return value of the target method as arguments:

    ```
    @AfterReturning(pointcut="execution(*
    com.spring_cookbook.controllers.*.*(..))",
    returning="returnValue")
    public void logReturnValue(JoinPoint joinPoint, Object
    returnValue) {
      ...
    }
    ```

2. In that advice method, log the return value preceded by the target method name:

    ```
    String className =
    joinPoint.getSignature().getDeclaringTypeName();
    String methodName = joinPoint.getSignature().getName();
    System.out.println("-----" + className + "." + methodName +
    "() -----");
    System.out.println("returnValue=" + returnValue);
    ```

3. Test the advice using a controller method that returns a value:

    ```
    @RequestMapping("user_list")
    @ResponseBody
    public String userList() {
      return "just a test";
    }
    ```

4. Check whether it's working. When going to /user_list in your browser, you should see the following in your server log:

```
-----
com.spring_cookbook.controllers.UserController.userList()
-----
returnValue=just a test
```

How it works...

The @AfterReturning annotation preceding the advice method is a pointcut expression:

```
@AfterReturning(pointcut="execution(*
com.spring_cookbook.controllers.*.*(..))",
returning="returnValue")
```

Refer to the *Measuring the execution time of methods using an around advice* recipe for more details. The returning attribute is the name of the argument of the advice method to be used for the return value.

 Note that if an exception is thrown during the execution of the target method, the after-returning advice won't be executed.

Logging exceptions using an after-throwing advice

An **after-throwing advice** executes some extra code when an exception is thrown during the execution of the target method. In this recipe, we will just log the exception.

Getting ready

We will use the aspect class defined in the *Creating a Spring AOP aspect class* recipe.

How to do it...

Here are the steps for logging an exception using an after-throwing advice:

1. In your aspect class, create an advice method annotated with @AfterThrowing. Make it take a JoinPoint object and an Exception object as arguments:

```
@AfterThrowing(pointcut="execution(*
com.spring_cookbook.controllers.*.*(..))",
throwing="exception")
```

```
public void logException(JoinPoint joinPoint, Exception
exception) {
    ...
}
```

2. In that advice method, log the exception preceded by the target method name:

```
String className =
joinPoint.getSignature().getDeclaringTypeName();
String methodName = joinPoint.getSignature().getName();
System.out.println("-----" + className + "." + methodName +
"() -----");
System.out.println("exception message:" +
exception.getMessage());
```

3. Test the advice using a controller method throwing an exception:

```
@RequestMapping("user_list")
@ResponseBody
public String userList() throws Exception {
    throw new Exception("a bad exception");
}
```

4. Check whether it's working. When going to /user_list in your browser, you should see the following in your server log:

```
-----
com.spring_cookbook.controllers.UserController.userList()
-----
exception message:a bad exception
```

How it works...

The @AfterThrowing annotation preceding the advice method is a pointcut expression:

```
@AfterThrowing(pointcut="execution(*
com.spring_cookbook.controllers.*.*(..))", throwing="exception")
```

Refer to the *Measuring the execution time of methods using an around advice* recipe for more details. The throwing attribute is the name of the argument of the advice method to be used for the exception object thrown by the target method.

 Note that if no exception is thrown during the execution of the target method, the after-throwing advice won't be executed.

Using an after advice to clean up resources

An **after advice** executes some extra code after the execution of the target method, even if an exception is thrown during its execution. Use this advice to clean up resources by removing a temporary file or closing a database connection. In this recipe, we will just log the target method name.

Getting ready

We will use the aspect class defined in the *Creating a Spring AOP aspect class* recipe.

How to do it...

Here are the steps for using an after advice:

1. In your aspect class, create an advice method annotated with `@After`. Make it take `JoinPoint` as an argument:

    ```
    @After("execution(*
    com.spring_cookbook.controllers.*.*(..))")
    public void cleanUp(JoinPoint joinPoint) {
    ...
    }
    ```

2. In that advice method, log the target method name:

    ```
    String className =
    joinPoint.getSignature().getDeclaringTypeName();
    String methodName = joinPoint.getSignature().getName();
    System.out.println("-----" + className + "." + methodName +
    "() -----");
    ```

3. Test the advice using two controller methods: one executes normally and the other one throws an exception:

    ```
    @RequestMapping("user_list")
    @ResponseBody
    public String userList() {
      return "method returning normally";
    }

    @RequestMapping("user_list2")
    @ResponseBody
    public String userList2() throws Exception  {
      throw new Exception("just a test");
    }
    ```

4. Check whether it's working. When going to /user_list or /user_list2 in your browser, you should see this in your server log:

```
-----
com.spring_cookbook.controllers.UserController.userList()
-----
```

How it works...

The @After annotation preceding the advice method is a pointcut expression:

```
@After("execution(* com.spring_cookbook.controllers.*.*(..))")
```

Refer to the *Measuring the execution time of methods using an around advice* recipe for more details.

Making a class implement an interface at runtime using an introduction

An **introduction** allows us to make a Java class (we will refer to it as the *target class*) implement an interface at runtime. With Spring AOP, introductions can be applied only to Spring beans (controllers, services, and so on). In this recipe, we will create an interface, its implementation, and make a Spring controller implement that interface at runtime using that implementation. To check whether it's working, we will also add a before advice to the controller method to execute a method from the interface implementation.

Getting ready

We will use the aspect class defined in the *Creating a Spring AOP aspect class* recipe.

How to do it...

Here are the steps for using an introduction:

1. Create the Logging interface:

```
public interface Logging {
  public void log(String str);
}
```

2. Create an implementation class for it:

```
public class LoggingConsole implements Logging {

  public void log(String str) {
```

```
          System.out.println(str);
    }
}
```

3. In your aspect class, add a `Logging` attribute annotated with `@DeclareParents`. Add the implementation class to `@DeclareParents`:

```
@DeclareParents(value =
"com.spring_cookbook.controllers.*+", defaultImpl =
LoggingConsole.class)
public static Logging mixin;
```

4. Add an advice method annotated with `@Before`. Make it take a `Logging` object as an argument:

```
@Before("execution(*
com.spring_cookbook.controllers.*.*(..)) && this(logging)")
public void logControllerMethod(Logging logging) {
    ...
}
```

5. In the advice method, use the `Logging` object:

```
logging.log("this is displayed just before a controller
method is executed.");
```

6. Test whether it's working with a standard controller method:

```
@RequestMapping("user_list")
@ResponseBody
public String userList() {
   return "method returning normally";
}
```

7. Check whether it's working. When going to `/user_list` in your browser, you should see the following in your server log:

```
this is displayed just before a controller method is
executed.
```

How it works...

In the aspect class, the `@DeclareParents` annotation preceding the Logging attribute is a pointcut expression:

```
@DeclareParents(value = "com.spring_cookbook.controllers.*+",
defaultImpl = LoggingConsole.class)
```

This pointcut expression and the `Logging` attribute define that:

- ▶ The introduction will be applied to all controller classes: `com.spring_cookbook.controllers.*+`
- ▶ The introduction will make these controller classes implement the Logging interface: `public static Logging mixin;`
- ▶ The introduction will make these controller classes use `LoggingConsole` as implementation of the Logging interface: `defaultImpl = LoggingConsole.class`

The before advice works the same way as in the *Measuring the execution time of methods using an around advice* recipe. It only takes one extra condition:

```
this(logging)
```

This means that the advice will be applied only to objects that implement the Logging interface.

Setting the execution order of the aspects

When using several aspect classes, it can be necessary to set the order in which the aspects are executed. In this recipe, we will use two aspect classes with before advices targeting controller methods.

Getting ready

We will use the configuration from the *Creating a Spring AOP aspect class* recipe.

We will use these two aspect classes containing an advice, which logs some text when it's executed:

```java
@Component
@Aspect
public class Aspect1 {

  @Before("execution(* com.spring_cookbook.controllers.*.*(..))")
  public void advice1() {
    System.out.println("advice1");
  }

}

@Component
@Aspect
```

```
public class Aspect2 {

  @Before("execution(* com.spring_cookbook.controllers.*.*(..))")
  public void advice2() {
    System.out.println("advice2");
  }

}
```

How to do it...

Here are the steps to set the execution order of the two aspect classes:

1. Add @Order with a number as parameter to the first aspect:

    ```
    @Component
    @Aspect
    @Order(1)
    public class Aspect1 {
    ```

2. Add @Order with another number as parameter to the second aspect:

    ```
    @Component
    @Aspect
    @Order(2)
    public class Aspect2 {
    ```

3. Test whether it's working. When going to /user_list in your browser, you should see this in your server log:

    ```
    advice1
    advice2
    ```

4. Switch the @Order numbers and check whether the execution order is changed:

    ```
    advice2
    advice1
    ```

How it works...

The aspects are executed in the ascending order set by @Order.

There's more...

It's not possible to set an order between advice methods of the same aspect class. If it becomes necessary, create new aspect classes for those advices.

Index

Symbols

@Autowired annotation
  bean, using 27
@Bean annotation
  bean, defining 24
@Component annotation
  bean, defining 25, 26
.mobi domain name
  using, on mobiles 148

A

advices 193
after advice
  used, for cleaning up resources 202, 203
after-returning advice
  used, for logging methods
      return values 199, 200
after-throwing advice
  used, for logging exceptions 200, 201
annotations
  used, for validating form 81, 82
API key 167
API secret 167
AppConfig configuration class
  about 16
  annotations 16
App ID 154
application context
  used, for unit testing with JUnit 4 108-110
  used, for unit testing with TestNG 6 110, 111
App secret 154
arguments, methods
  logging, before advice used 197, 198

around advice
  used, for measuring execution time
      of methods 195-197
AspectJ 193
aspect-oriented programming (AOP) 193
aspects
  about 193
  execution order, setting 205, 206
attributes
  passing from controller method,
      to JSP view 36
authenticated users
  page elements, displaying 97

B

batch job 117, 118
bean
  about 23
  defining, explicitly with @Bean 24
  defining, implicitly with @Component 25, 26
  initialization 26
  listing 29
  name, customizing 24, 25
  name, setting 28
  reference link 26
  retrieving 29
  using 23
  using, directly 28
  using, via dependency injection 27
before advice
  used, for logging method
      arguments 197, 198

C

checkbox
using 76
class
interface implementing, with
introduction 203-205
command line
job, executing from 122-124
common prefix
using, for routes 37
constraint annotations
@Max(120) 83
@Min(18) 83
@NotBlank 83
@NotEmpty 83
@NotNull 83
@Valid 83
reference link 83
controller class
DAO method, calling 53
controller method
argument used, for retrieving submitted
form value 69
attributes passing, to JSP view 36
common prefix, using for routes 37
dynamic route parameters, using 36
execution time measuring, around
advice used 195-197
job, executing from 124, 125
route, associating 33
unit testing 112-115
controllers
code executing, interceptors used 43, 44
CSV file
generating 136, 137
custom login page
used, for authenticating users 91-93

D

DAO (data access object) class
creating 52
DAO method
calling, from controller class 53
list of objects, retrieving 56

list of objects, retrieving with their
dependencies 57-59
list of objects, saving 61
umber of results, finding for SQL query 60
object, retrieving 55
object, saving 53, 54
object, updating 59
database
connection, performing 50, 51
reading from 138, 139
reference link 50
used, for authenticating users 93-95
default login page
used, for authenticating users 89, 90
dependency injection
bean, using 27
using 23
domain name
using, on mobiles 150
dynamic route parameters
using, in controller method 36

E

Eclipse
about 1
installing, on Mac OS 4
installing, on Ubuntu 8
installing, on Windows 12
URL 4
exceptions
logging, after-throwing advice used 200, 201
Expression Language (EL) 36
expressions, Spring
URL 98

F

Facebook
connecting to 157-160
custom object, posting 165, 166
link, posting 164
status update, posting 163
URL, for developer account 154
user's friends list, retrieving 162
user's profile, retrieving 160, 161

Facebook app
  creating 154, 155
file
  uploading 83-85
form
  data, saving in object 71, 72
  default values, setting with
      model object 70, 71
  displaying 68, 69
  processing 68, 69
  validating, annotations used 81, 82
FreeMarker 35

H

Hessian 184
Hessian service
  creating 184, 185
  querying 186, 187
Hibernate
  about 49
  used, for object persistence 62-64
  used, for querying 62, 63
hidden fields
  using 72, 73
HTTP Invoker 180
HTTP Invoker service
  creating 180-182
  querying 182, 183
HTTPS
  about 87
  using, with Tomcat 99, 100

I

incomplete database modifications
  reverting, transactions used 61, 62
interceptors
  used, for executing code 43, 44
introduction
  used, for interface implementation in
      class 203-205

J

Java
  about 1
  installing, on Mac OS 2

installing, on Ubuntu 5
installing, on Windows 8-10
reference link, for downloading 2, 9
Java Database Connectivity (JDBC) 49
Java Persistence API (JPA)
  URL 63
Java RMI 176
Java RMI service
  creating 176-178
  querying 179, 180
job
  creating 120-122
  executing, from command line 122-124
  executing, from controller method 124, 125
  parameters, using 126
  scheduling 127-129
Job Execution 118
Job Instance 118
join point 197
JSON 188
JSP files
  organizing, with subfolders 41
  reference link 35
JSP view
  attributes passing, from controller method 36
  using 34, 35
  using, for mobiles 147
JUnit
  about 102
  method annotations 103
JUnit 4
  unit testing 102, 103
  unit testing, Springs application
      context used 108-110

L

List<Object>
  using 76
list of checkboxes
  using 77, 78
list of objects
  retrieving 56
  retrieving, with their dependencies 57-59
  saving 61
list of radio buttons
  using 79, 80

resources
cleaning up, after advice used 202, 203
REST API 188
REST service
creating 188-190
querying 191, 192
route
associating, to controller method 33
common prefix, using 37

S

Secure Sockets Layer (SSL) 87
select field
List<Object>, using 76
List<String> object, using 75
using 73, 74
Spring AOP
aspect class, creating 194, 195
Spring Batch
configuring 119, 120
installing 119, 120
URL 120
Spring Mobile
installing 142
Spring Security
enabling 88, 89
Spring web application
"Hello World" web page, creating 15, 16
configuration classes, creating 14-16
creating 13
Maven project, creating in Eclipse 13-15
running 17
Spring, adding to project 13-16
SQL query
number of results, finding 60
standard Java application
building, Spring used 18-21
configuration class, creating 19
Maven project, creating in Eclipse 18
Spring, adding to project 19
User class, creating 19
User singleton, defining 20
User singleton, using 20, 21
Step Execution 118
subfolder path
using, on mobiles 151, 152

submitted form value
retrieving, controller method argument
used 69
system command
executing 126, 127

T

tablets
detecting 143, 144
test Facebook app
creating 156
TestNG
about 104
method annotations 106
references 106
TestNG 6
unit testing 104-106
unit testing, Springs application
context used 110, 111
test users
creating 156
text
using 72, 73
text attribute
used, for defining page titles 42
textarea
using 72, 73
Thymeleaf 35
Tiles
page template, using 38-41
reference link 42
Tomcat
about 1
executing, on Mac OS 5
executing, on Ubuntu 8
HTTPS, using 99, 100
installing, on Mac OS 4
installing, on Ubuntu 7
installing, on Windows 12
URL 4
tools, for Spring development
Eclipse 1
Java 1
Maven 1
Tomcat 1

transactions

　used, for reverting incomplete database
　　modifications 61, 62

　used, for unit testing 111

Twitter

　connecting to 167-171

　URL 167

　user's profile, retrieving 172

　application, creating 167

Twitter user

　private message, sending 174

　tweet, posting 173, 174

　tweets, retrieving 173

U

Ubuntu

　Eclipse, installing 8

　Java, installing 5

　Maven, installing 6

　Tomcat, installing 7

unit testing

　controller methods 112-116

　URL, for naming convention 103

　with JUnit 4 102, 103

　with JUnit 4, Springs application context
　　used 108-110

　with TestNG 6 104-106

　with TestNG 6, Springs application context
　　used 110, 111

　with transactions 111

unit testing batch jobs 139, 140

User-Agent header 144

user authentication 87

user authorization 87

users

　authenticating, custom login page
　　used 91-93

　authenticating, database used 93-95

　authenticating, default login page
　　used 89, 90

　authorizing, with specific role 97

V

Velocity 35

W

Windows

　Eclipse, installing 12

　Java, installing 8-10

　Maven, installing 10-12

　Tomcat, installing 12

X

XML file

　reading 134-136

Thank you for buying
Spring Cookbook

About Packt Publishing

Packt, pronounced 'packed', published its first book, *Mastering phpMyAdmin for Effective MySQL Management*, in April 2004, and subsequently continued to specialize in publishing highly focused books on specific technologies and solutions.

Our books and publications share the experiences of your fellow IT professionals in adapting and customizing today's systems, applications, and frameworks. Our solution-based books give you the knowledge and power to customize the software and technologies you're using to get the job done. Packt books are more specific and less general than the IT books you have seen in the past. Our unique business model allows us to bring you more focused information, giving you more of what you need to know, and less of what you don't.

Packt is a modern yet unique publishing company that focuses on producing quality, cutting-edge books for communities of developers, administrators, and newbies alike. For more information, please visit our website at www.packtpub.com.

About Packt Open Source

In 2010, Packt launched two new brands, Packt Open Source and Packt Enterprise, in order to continue its focus on specialization. This book is part of the Packt open source brand, home to books published on software built around open source licenses, and offering information to anybody from advanced developers to budding web designers. The Open Source brand also runs Packt's open source Royalty Scheme, by which Packt gives a royalty to each open source project about whose software a book is sold.

Writing for Packt

We welcome all inquiries from people who are interested in authoring. Book proposals should be sent to author@packtpub.com. If your book idea is still at an early stage and you would like to discuss it first before writing a formal book proposal, then please contact us; one of our commissioning editors will get in touch with you.

We're not just looking for published authors; if you have strong technical skills but no writing experience, our experienced editors can help you develop a writing career, or simply get some additional reward for your expertise.

Spring Security [Video]

ISBN: 978-1-78216-865-2   Duration: 02:10 hours

An empirical approach to securing your web applications

1. Fully secure your web application with Spring Security.

2. Implement authentication and registration with the database as well as with LDAP.

3. Utilize authorization examples that help guide you through the authentication of users step-by-step.

Spring Security 3.1

ISBN: 978-1-84951-826-0   Paperback: 456 pages

Secure your web applications from hackers with this step-by-step guide

1. Learn to leverage the power of Spring Security to keep intruders at bay through simple examples that illustrate real world problems.

2. Each sample demonstrates key concepts allowing you to build your knowledge of the architecture in a practical and incremental way.

3. Filled with samples that clearly illustrate how to integrate with the technologies and frameworks of your choice.

Please check **www.PacktPub.com** for information on our titles

Printed in Germany
by Amazon Distribution
GmbH, Leipzig